Yiasou Ikaria

Stories, Myth and Poem
About a Very Peculiar Greek Island

Ikaria, sitting almost in the middle of the Aegean Sea, shaped like a crooked finger pointing accusingly at Turkey, has been stereotyped as a backwater Greek island for ages. Maybe, because of this, Ikarians developed into a proud, but also strange and almost exotic group of islanders as labeled by their fellow Greeks.

"Yiasou Ikaria" is a collection of short vignettes featuring an assortment of unusual, charming characters who find themselves in bizarre and hilarious situations, defining what a true Ikarian is. So grab your favorite Greek beverage, an ouzo, a frappe, or a potent coffee and spend some time on this uniquely Greek island with its equally entertaining cast of characters.

Dimitri Mantakounis

Chapbook Press

Schuler Books
2660 28th Street SE
Grand Rapids, MI 49512
(616) 942-7330
www.schulerbooks.com

Yiasou Ikaria: Stories, Myth and Poem About a Very Peculiar Greek Island

ISBN 13: 9781943359455

Library of Congress Control Number: 2016953796

Copyright © 2016, Dimitri Mantakounis

Cover art by Kemon Lardas

All rights reserved.

No part of this book may be reproduced in any form without express permission of the copyright holder.

Printed in the United States by Chapbook Press.

To Andrea:

The most beautiful daughter

Hater of adjectives

Inimitable Koukla

Love Dad

TABLE OF CONTENTS

DAMN IT THE SUN WILL MELT YOUR WINGS 1
GIRL IN A STEEL TANK 2
BEER RUN 4
STUBBED TOES, BRUISED EGOS 6
AGIOS KIRIKOS 8
WHAT GARBAGE? 9
SWALLOWS 11
IKARIAN OBSERVATIONS 13
REALLY? 14
GARBAGE TRUCK 16
CLAW MACHINE 18
WHAT WAS THAT?? 19
SHOPPING IN IKARIA 21
CONTRADICTIONS 23
WHAT A DAY (A MYTH) 25
TRAVELS WITH DAD PART I 27
TRAVELS WITH DAD PART II 33
TRAVELS WITH DAD PART III 37
THE NEW AIRPORT 40
FLYING TO IKARIA 42
THE ONE EURO STORE 44
WHERE'S THE MONEY FROM? 45
SALES SLIPS AND TAXES 47
THE LOTTERY 49
THE LADY BUYS A WEAPON 51
OTE 53
IT DID WHAT? 54
NOW WHO'S MACHO? 56
IKARIA, JULY 1970 59
POKING DEATH WITH A STICK 61
HOW POLITICAL IS YOUR BEER? 66
ONE MORE FORM… 68
AGIOS KIRIKOS II 71
THREE CHAIRS AND A TABLE 75

DAMN IT THE SUN WILL MELT YOUR WINGS

Ikaria, when I mention the name most people will just shrug, then I explain that Ikaria is part of a famous ancient Greek myth. It concerns a father and son who secretly escaped imprisonment from Crete after fashioning wings made from feathers and wax. The father's instructions to his son, Ikaros, were not to fly too high or the sun's rays would melt his wings. The brash son disregarded his father's advice and the outcome was he crashed into the Aegean Sea, near the island that consequently was named after him, Ikaria.

The story is a myth but the island is not. Located in the eastern Aegean, it is a rather long, skinny island with a somewhat dubious history, encompassed in a beautiful and provoking topography. It truly reflects what Lawrence Durrell describes as, "spirit of place." A peoples' spirit that evolves from being geographically isolated, politically defaulted, and culturally insulated. A spirit that promotes self-sufficiency, an almost arrogant island view and a watchful and suspicious eye towards outsiders.

It was on this wayward island that I was born in the middle of the 20th century in a mountain village said to have existed since the Stone Age. Having left this quaint existence at the age of five, I returned many years later to reacclimatize myself to my heritage on this lonely and windy island. During countless summers spent exploring and eventually settling down as a permanent part-time resident, I amassed vivid memories and experiences of the people and places of Ikaria. This shared life compels me to tell the stories of these Ikarians, to illuminate their experiences and provide a viewing window into the human spirits that inhabit this majestically rocky island called Ikaria.

GIRL IN A STEEL TANK

Living on Ikaria, especially during the dry summer months requires one to be duly concerned about water conservation and usage. The fresh water supply is controlled by the local entities and in our situation by the village water authorities. As such, they try to regulate and conserve as much water as possible during these arid periods. Most locals have some kind of water reservoir placed on the roof of their homes. These reservoirs can hold anywhere from about fifty gallons to several hundred gallons of water, depending on their size and shape.

We also had a reservoir perched on top of our roof, one made of metal, painted bright green (I don't know why) by my father. The life span of such a metal box before it tends to rust out and leak water all over the roof is determined by how well it is maintained. Since the water entering the reservoir comes directly from the mountains, it is unfiltered and contains small amounts of dirt and sand, that through time accumulate at the bottom of the cistern. About once a year or so this sediment needs to be removed. One would assume some kind of flushing mechanism would be installed in the water tanks, but no, that was not the case with our tank, that would be too convenient. In order to clean out the insides, the flow to the tank would have to be turned off, and all the retained water would have to be drained, leaving a few inches of water in the bottom along with the build-up. This presents a problem of how to remove the accumulated watery grime. The top opening of our tank was no bigger than the size of a regular manila folder. It would be pried open then someone would stick a mop in thru the opening slush around the remaining water and sediment and hope that most of it would exit out the outflow pipe.

This was not a very effective way of debris removal as my plumber, Niko remarked the day he came to clean out the tank. Jokingly, he suggested a better way would be to have a small person in the tank with a mop and sponge to soak up all the water and sediment. Taking his peculiar suggestion literally, my mind immediately flashed to the only individual diminutive enough to fit through the small opening, my eight-year-old daughter, Andrea. It took some coaxing and assurances that there were no snakes, lizards, or other such creepy monsters inhabiting the dark and spooky water tank. I reassured her the plumber and I would be outside the tank at all times, holding flashlights and shining the way for her. After a few moments of deep thought and the possibility of acquiring another Barbie doll for her collection, Andrea gallantly agreed to this unusual plumbing experiment.

Lifting her up over the metal opening I slowly lowered her into the foreboding, green, watery repository, while the disbelieving plumber shined a rather dim light into the cavernous tank. I handed her a bucket, a sponge, and a mop. Cautiously, I coached her to crawl from corner to corner removing the damp sediment. In less than fifteen minutes, either out of fear or claustrophobia, she emerged clutching the bucket in her little hands, and reeking of dampness. Her bathing suit, once a brilliant Barbie pink, now crusted over with mud, was the shade of bubble gum infused with chocolate syrup. Happily though, she acknowledged the bravery she exhibited in the daunting feat of cleaning out the disgusting water tank. It wasn't till later that same afternoon that she emphatically swore on a pile of Barbies that she would never go into that tank again.

To this very day in the kafenion around our village, the story of the brave eight-year-old girl, who was lowered into and cleaned out a damp, dirty water tank is still being told by a retired plumber, while thinking out loud to himself, "What is wrong with her father?"

BEER RUN

It's no secret to anyone who knows me, that like many men, I enjoy a cold frosty beer on a hot day, and certainly there are plenty of hot days during the scorching summer months in Ikaria. The problem arises, as it does everywhere, when the beer runs out. This of course means that someone has to make the all-important beer run. In Ikaria, as in most parts of Greece, acquiring alcohol is as easy as buying a can of Coke. This is because of Greece's favorable and tolerant drinking laws. For a long time at our seaside village, the only places to buy beer were the kafenios, our diminutive grocery store or the one-man bakery that sold three items, bread, beer and tiropites. The closest of the three sites to our house was the bakery, about a half kilometer away. However, it meant taking the rocky foot path, past the sweet smelling bushes full of bees, avoiding the ever present goats that often blocked the path and traversing around the noisy and odorous chicken coops.

This daunting but essential undertaking was always hotly contested by everyone, because it meant a fairly arduous uphill walk to the bakery and back again carrying multiple bottles of cold beer. The task was usually assigned to one of the younger members of my family, either my son, Alex, or my daughter Andrea. Since Andrea was the younger of the two, her brother somehow mysteriously conned her, along with lucrative bribes from me, into taking the trek up to the bakery. This brave six-year-old would take her little pink backpack and start her odyssey hoping to avoid the many perils along the way. Under ideal conditions we could expect her back in about half an hour with her bag full of liquid refreshments. This common practice of allowing minors to purchase beer for their parents fit perfectly into the lifestyle of the island. My wife and I certainly had no qualms about sending our children on these quests for beer, that is until we returned to the States.

Back in the States one of the most popular classroom activities for first graders was the weekly show and tell, not only for the students but also for teachers. Six-year-old Andrea, having traveled to Ikaria three times in her short life, always had plenty to show and tell about life on the island, especially one week when the topic was farm animals. When it was Andrea's turn to tell about animals in her life she stood up with bravado to explain to her fellow classmates and her teacher, how she had to take these dangerous journeys to the village bakery in order to bring back beer for her thirsty parents. She described in vivid detail how she had to circumnavigate the bee bushes so as not to get stung, how she had to out maneuver the intimidating and stubborn goats, and how she had to hold her breath as she quickly passed the smelly chicken coop. The toughest part of her odyssey she explained to her class, was carrying those heavy chilled bottles of beer in her little pink Barbie back pack. The weight of the hefty bottles often threw her off balance landing her in the thicket and brush resulting in scratches or bruises, as she made her descent from   the bakery along the uneven rocky foot path.

When Andrea came home from school that afternoon she told us about her school day and the electrifying story she told during show and tell. My wife and I immediately knew and understood the predicament we were in. Did her teacher believe her? Or maybe she thought Andrea made up the story? Would her teacher call Child Protective Services on us for child abuse, negligence or endangerment? Luckily no authorities came knocking on our door, no phone calls asking if we'd be available for a home visit. However, at parent-teacher conferences later that year I couldn't help but notice a certain amount of probing and suspicious looks from Andrea's teacher. The looks that mean: "I'm not quite sure what is going on with your strange and unusual family, but if Andrea comes to school with beer breath I have Protective Services on speed dial."

STUBBED TOES, BRUISED EGOS

Topping off the list of natural wonders on Ikaria is the diversity of beautiful and exotic beaches. Some are tucked out-of-the-way secluded beaches others are umbrella laced sandy beaches stretching for several kilometers. The north side of the island has the fine white to gray sandy beaches, that one can find in semi-tropical places like Florida. The south side however, is rutted with numerous beaches made up with everything from giant boulders to small pebbles. They are round and smooth, made of quartz, basalt or marble.

Negotiating such a beach setting becomes quite a Herculean effort for those used to granular type beaches of let's say California or the Great Lakes. One fascinating activity for me to watch is the first time beachgoer getting around the slippery rocky beaches.

What follows is a typical entry and exit into and out of the Aegean waters. Leaving the cool shade of the sea pines, the first obstacle one faces is how to overcome the scorching heat radiating from the stones that have been baked all day by the Greek sun. Some sort of footwear is definitely required as to not burn one's feet. As one carefully walks to the water's edge, the footwear is removed, and immediately one is confronted with the wet, slippery rocks. Now, extreme balance is required to enter the water without falling on one's face, or turning an ankle in a desperate maneuver of water access. There are only two options for this tricky entry. Very popular with the young is the macho dive, in which one takes running leaps to the edge of the water. They run so fast that their feet never seem to touch the hot rocks. When the water looks barely deep enough to be safe, they dive head first into the chilly Aegean. Using this technique one avoids having to traverse the rocky bottom. Then there is the exact opposite, the calculated creep, usually employed by the older crowd. Here one cautiously and methodically approaches the water, gingerly enters while trying to maintain balance on the treacherous rocks. When comfortable enough, one submerges their torso into the refreshing water, trying desperately to dodge splashing children and knock-you down waves.

After enjoying a cool swim in the Aegean, the arduous task of exiting commences. One's first attempt might be to waddle out of the water like a duck, pushing up the rocky incline. With arms flailing wildly, one quickly realizes walking on just heels makes one slip back in the water, with no traction, and guarantees the of stubbing of a toe or two. Another type of exiting is the salamander walk. Basically this requires one to bend over and crawl out of the water on all fours. This makes one look like an early amphibian crawling out of the primeval ooze. This technique, ungraceful as it is, will work if there are no waves, or else one will be repeatedly pelted in the face by the constant watery action. Sometimes walking backwards out of the water works, but then not being able to see behind oneself is a hazard. Slipping on a slick, algae covered rock and ending up on one's derriere is a high probability.

The best way of exiting, to me, seems that one should stand erect, slightly bent at the waist, using only the toes and balls of the feet, with arms spread out for balance. Take small steady steps towards dry land, while looking down in front to navigate around any obstacles. Once on shore, one's immediate instinct is to dart quickly back to the shade of the sea pines. Moving expeditiously over the searing rocks you arrive at your sheltered destination only to look around, realizing disappointedly that your sandals are at the edge of the water, twenty-five scorching meters away.

AGIOS KIRIKOS

Agios Kirikos, the capital of Ikaria, or Agios as locals call it is for the most part a sleepy, little harbor town, but on at least one occasion it exhibited a rather unique cultural flavor. One morning as I arrived at Agios to do my every-other day shopping, I heard some very faint non-native sounds. In the main square I happened upon a group of Ikarians gathered in a circle. Coming from the center of this crowd I could hear the music and beating of what sounded like Native American drums. Inside this cluster of about fifty or so Ikarians was indeed a dance troupe of four Native American Indians dressed in an eclectic wardrobe of Plains/Woodland Indians. They exuberantly danced around a table waving their fringed tomahawks in the air and yelling war cries to the beat of their drums. The stunned Ikarians looked bewildered and confused, as did I, as to what this dance program was about.

Upon finishing their dance number, the Indians proceeded to pass around a hat for donations. As the hat was circulating among the amused onlookers the performers brought out CD's of their music to be sold to the locals. Out of curiosity I approached one of the dancers to find out what tribe they were from since I did not recognize the outfits they wore. With a whimsical smile the oldest male dancer said, "We're not American Indians, we're from Ecuador. We just put these shows on because Greeks only know about Indians from American western TV shows." So, cultural exchange programs do happen even in remote destinations such as Agios. The question becomes what culture?

WHAT GARBAGE?

As so often happens among Aegean islands, small squabbles, usually concerning fishing, politics or who has the best dancers, emerge, are highlighted for a while, and then dissipate over the Aegean Sea. Occasionally though, an unusual crisis crops up and takes center stage as it did on Ikaria in 2012. With Ikaria entering the disposable material age years ago, one could no longer burn tidy little bags of garbage in ones back yard, and with the increase of tourist every summer, the amount of garbage exceeded the local capacity to handle the overflow. The Ikarian officials invested in new Mercedes Benz garbage trucks, put out a variety of bins to collect recyclables, and opened up a dump in the middle of the island to deal with the abundance of discarded rubbish. Slowly though, the dump filled up and could no longer handle the constant arrival and dumping of the garbage trucks, and was forced to close. This presented a dilemma for the local officials as the bins brimmed over, and the garbage started to pile up in the streets.

Sometime during the discussions of what to do with this aggregate of trash, a decision was reached by the local authorities to pile the garbage onto a barge and take it somewhere, but where? The approved suggestion was to secretly, in the dark of night, float this barge to the neighboring islands of Fourni. Since the islands are sparsely populated, there would be ample room to accommodate the ever increasing collection of trash from Ikaria.

The garbage was quickly gathered and loaded onto an enormous barge and deployed for its' two-hour trip to Fourni.

The secrecy of this mission unfortunately was compromised when the locals on Fourni, hearing from an inside source, of the covert Ikarian operation, mounted their own stealth counterattack. There to meet the phantom barge, in the dead of night, was a delegation of Fournotes, who adamantly forced the unwanted and malodorous barge to turn around and make a hasty retreat back to Ikaria.

Stuck with this smelly barge, authorities once again met to decide the outcome of this traveling garbage pile. In the meantime, Ikarians were becoming irritated with the slow progress of the garbage issue, and public resentment resonated across the island. Finally, after weeks and much consternation, negotiations by the local authorities were completed for the acceptance of the barge by another neighboring island. This island, seeing the profitable silver lining in the Ikarian trash, demanded payment up front in order to take in the garbage for the rest of the year. So, if by chance you are island hopping around the Aegean Sea be sure to keep a lookout for the floating garbage pile, but then again you probably will smell it before you see it.

SWALLOWS

Swallows don't just return to Capistrano, they also return to our little seaside eatery in Xilosirti, Ikaria. Earlier in the summer, a pair of swallows found themselves flying through the wide open windows and doors of our local restaurant.

As they flew nonchalantly in and out of the dining room, to their feathery amazement they discovered the ideal perch on which to build their snug little nest. This perch just happened to be located on top of a light fixture that was hanging precariously in the middle of the restaurant. Oblivious to the noise and crowds of the restaurant, the unconventional birds arduously built their tiny mud nest, and quickly produced three bird eggs. Within weeks three diminutive chick heads were seen bobbing up and down in the nest with their beaks perpetually wide open. The parent swallows continued to make frequent forays in and out of the restaurant gathering sustenance for their young stock.

The owners of the restaurant, as well as the customers became quite accustomed to the new tenants and their low flying aerial antics. Tourists and locals from all over the island came to eat at the restaurant just so they could witness and take pictures of the frolicking birds. Many of us became bird watching addicts, popping in every day to get the latest report as to the health and well-being of the chicks. Quite often we noticed one of the bird parents stoically perched on top of the huge flat screen TV that was fastened to the wall at the far end of the restaurant. The bird casually observing the hustle and bustle of the busy eatery as patrons filtered in and out till the early morning hours. To protect customers from the bird droppings, tables were re-arranged and a large piece of cardboard placed on the floor under the light fixture that supported the celebrated bird nest. Customers and wait staff avoided that part of the restaurant, but during one exciting Euro Cup match, a patron celebrating the winning goal in his enthusiasm, stood up, jumped around, stepped on the bird poop laden cardboard and slid half way across the restaurant. Customers witnessing this amazing gymnastic feat applauded his dexterity and keen sense of balance thunderously; all the while the birds seemed unimpressed by the wild gyrations of the soccer fan.

By the end of the summer two of the three birdies survived and fledged, hopefully to return the next summer and roost in the same nest, still attached to the dangling light fixture, and once again to entertain and delight customers with their aerial acrobatics.

I couldn't help but wonder how quickly the swallows, their chicks, and their nest would be forcibly evicted if this aviary incident took place in the States. No sooner would you utter the words, "Big Bird", then the health department would materialize with hazard suites, oxygen tanks, and gallons of disinfectant to rid the Aves intruders. Ikarians for the most part take a more amicable St. Francis approach towards birds, sympathetic and compassionate, that's why I hope to see swallows flying around my neighborhood for a long, long time.

IKARIAN OBSERVATIONS

MULTITASKING: IKARIAN STYLE

All of us in this busy world are called upon to perform many tasks, sometimes simultaneously. Ikarians are no exceptions. It is not uncommon to see Ikarians shopping, carrying on a conversation and driving at the same time. One young Ikarian took this to extremes when I noticed him riding his Harley motorcycle, cigarette in mouth, plastic cup of coffee in one hand and talking on his cell phone with the other. Nonchalantly motoring his way down the streets of Agios, everything in perfect balance, multitasking Ikarian style.

SIGNS

Signs for the most part inform, give advice, warn of danger and are generally seen by most of us as useful and on occasion intrusive. On Ikaria, one is never quite sure what signs mean or for whom they are intended. Walking into the National Bank of Greece at Agios Kirikos, customers are greeted by a variety of no smoking signs and warnings. These are plastered on the doors, the walls and on the tellers' windows. What seems apparent to most customers however, is not so apparent to the bank employees. Every other employee seems to be busy smoking, huffing and puffing, creating a permanent floating blue haze over the teller windows. I asked a bank employee about the no smoking signs and with a pretentious sneer and a whiff from his tobacco breath he informed me that the no smoking policy is meant for the bank customers only, and not the bank employees.

MECHANICS OF IKARIA

Owning a car in Ikaria is an expensive proposition. It's difficult to find qualified mechanics and there are long waits for parts to be shipped, so naturally if something goes wrong with their cars, most Ikarians attempt repairing their autos themselves. I was anointed with such a vision one dark evening in front of my house as two young men worked on a car. Apparently neither man had a flashlight, a lit candle was held by one man over the engine compartment, while the other, smoking a cigarette, worked on the motor. I chose at that moment not to hang around, fearing the combination of gas fumes, oil sludge, lit candle and cigarette were creating a massive potential for a catastrophe, not exactly a healthy life style choice.

REALLY?

As usual, things are not what they seem to be on Ikaria. There are even times when your eyes or other senses just can't logically be trusted to interpret the reality of a situation. We even joke about it saying "Don't believe anything you hear and only half of what you see." A situation that best illustrates this point happened when an American family was visiting us one summer a few years ago...

The family consisted of mom, dad and two kids, a girl around ten and her brother who had just turned five. Soon after they arrived at our house the young lad came down with a sore throat and a fever. Getting sick in Greece is a constant worry for travelers and locals alike. The socialized model of Greek medicine has its many benefits, but hospitals are sparse and vary in degree of medical care, and physician competency sometimes is questionable. After much family discussion it was decided that I should accompany the father and ill boy to our small hospital, as I was the host and the ever present translator. As it happened our hospital did have a pediatrician on staff, and as we registered the young patient, I requested an appointment with him. Since our American guests were not Greek citizens, or registered under the socialized medical umbrella, we were informed by the receptionist that they would have to pay cash to see the physician. She also indicated it would be over a thousand drachmas to see the doctor. With a strong dollar that summer the doctor bill came out to an astonishing $6.50. Being paying customers our wait was relatively short, and we were quickly ushered into the pediatrician's office. The first indication that something was not quite right occurred immediately

as we walked through the office door, and the odor of tobacco invaded our olfactory sense. As we took our seats in front of the doctor's desk, a desk filled and overflowing with patient charts, papers and other medical paraphernalia, we spotted a large dinner plate size ashtray brimming with half smoked cigarettes. A couple cigs were still smoldering, their light blue smoke slowly making the journey upward to the smoke tinged ceiling. Within minutes entered this young but serious looking doctor with a recently lit cigarette dangling precariously from his lips. Introductions were quickly made and symptoms of the illness discussed and diagnosed. During this brief dialogue none of us could take our eyes off the lit cigarette still well balanced and firmly attached to the young doctor's lips, as if an appendage was somehow permanently planted on the right side of his mouth.

Eventually the doctor had to physically examine the young patients' mouth, throat and take his temperature, and as duty called he did remove the half smoked cigarette from his mouth and deposit it on the ever growing Vesuvius mound of stale and smoldering tobacco. The nefarious strep throat was immediately diagnosed by the pediatrician, and a prescription for penicillin quickly written for the patient. As we headed for the pharmacy the conversation promptly revolved around the callous smoking behavior of this Greek doctor. Granted Greeks are the number one smokers in the EU, but one would assume that Greek medical practitioners, particularly ones that deal with children, acknowledge the health hazards and pitfalls of cigarette smoking. They should be promoting healthy life style choices and practices, but this being Ikaria, really, one shouldn't believe anything they hear and only half of what they see.

GARBAGE TRUCK

The rumors ran rampant, did Agios and the surrounding villages really get a garbage truck? Would our garbage really be picked up biweekly? If this was true that meant no longer having to burn our trash on calm windless days, or having to dig a hole and bury it, or sneaking our garbage to Agios and depositing it in the trash barrels of local businesses. Sure enough one quiet summer morning the ominous rumblings of a large vehicle could be heard in the far distance. As the noise drew closer I looked out my screen door to see a bright, new, orange and chrome Mercedes-Benz garbage truck, the Aegean sun bouncing off its polished veneer, slowly snaking its way down our narrow village streets. That's when I noticed a solitary figure sitting or rather straddling freestyle on top of this huge colossus of a truck. In his hands he held a large, menacing looking chainsaw, the kind you expect to see in one of those chainsaw horror movies. As the truck lumbered forward he would yell instructions to the driver to stop, thus allowing him to cut away any unsuspecting tree branches that would dare wreak havoc on the finish of the new Mercedes-Benz garbage truck. Yes, twice a week the roar of the garbage truck, sans scratches, could be heard as it made its way down our road picking up our trash, gnawing and grinding it to bits. To my amusement I would tell, like a proud father, to my friends back in the States that our little village not only has a garbage truck, but a brand new, sweet ass Mercedes-Benz garbage truck.

It didn't take long for the fascination of the new garbage truck to catch on, but its regular schedule route seemed to be in jeopardy because of logistic and parking concerns. Parking on the village's two streets is always a baffling and dauntless experience. Any car can easily block the minuscule roads if it is not properly parked and oriented in just the right angle and distance from the road. When this happens the garbage truck becomes blocked and can't proceed to make its pickups. The result of this impasse would be a very long and loud horn blast from the truck informing those whose vehicles were blocking the street to make haste and quickly move their offending cars.

A cautionary example of such a scene was played out one afternoon as I was returning home following our Mercedes-Benz garbage truck up one of the narrow and winding roads. Stopping suddenly, the truck was halted by an incorrectly parked car. The car was like a clog in the drain, the truck could not squeeze past the vehicle without falling off the road into the bramble below. The perpetrating auto did not have the two necessary tires parked on the sidewalk, so as to allow adequate space for the passage of other vehicles. Within seconds a host of cars, trucks, and three wheelers quickly jammed up behind us, horns blasting constantly in hopes of alleviating the traffic grid lock, but to no avail. The delinquent operator was nowhere to be seen. In a fit of desperate frustration, the garbage truck driver and his helper emerged from the cab of the truck and looked around for some able bodied men. Their glance caught my eye and my two fellow passengers. With a swift and determined downward wave of the drivers' hand, he signaled for our arguable assistance. Waiting for us at the illegally parked car, the garbage truck driver motioned for us to take a position behind the car, while he and his beefy helper would take care of the front of the vehicle. Upon the driver's command the five of us in unison lifted the vehicle as one lifts a pillow, and seamlessly moved it about a meter, depositing it next to an adjoining wall. With the road now clear, our entourage led by the magnificent and glowing Mercedes-Benz garbage truck continued on its' appointed route.

CLAW MACHINE

Coming into Agios it seems there is always a surprise waiting to amuse. This particular occurrence appeared on the main square where a carnival claw machine had spontaneously sprung up. This is a money munching machine in which a coin is deposited bringing a short period of time to maneuver the metal claw to grab a stuffed toy before time is up and the claw drops. If your aim is true and with a little bit of luck, you could grab one of those furry little creatures. Well, for Ikarians cute stuffed animals and the like are not a rewarding challenge for their half Euro coin. As I walked past the ominous looking claw machine I noticed a few stuffed animals were there, strategically placed, but to make the claw machine more enticing to the customers, it also included were the following items; several pairs of designer sunglasses and watches, (no doubt knockoffs), a Hello Kitty purse, whiskey flasks, several packs of possibly stale Marlboro Reds, and a box of condoms. These appealing and eclectic prizes were available to anyone, man, woman or child who had the coins and the spirit to take on the claw machine.

WHAT WAS THAT??

The topography of Ikaria is similar to most other Aegean islands, mountainous with several imposing peaks reaching over 1,000 meters in height. Needless to say traveling by auto around the island is a white knuckle experience. One follows the mountain terrain traversing corkscrew roads often doing switchbacks, and progressing at the speed of a tractor that requires constant shifting and braking. I always find myself with a feeling of great satisfaction when I can shift into third gear even if it is only for a fraction of a minute, maybe covering a grand distance of fifty meters or so. Such terrain provides for a variety of activities, which includes occasional military maneuvers by the Greek army.

Once again I found myself in a hurry on my red Vespa going from Xilocirtis to Agios to pick up my wife's birthday torte as quickly as possible before it melted in the 100-degree heat. Rounding one of the numerous bends in the road, I stumbled upon a detachment of young Greek soldiers huddled near their jeep under the shade of a large oak tree outside the yerokomio, relaxing and enjoying the national past time of Greeks, the compulsive obsession with political discourse. Continuing on my errand I raised my hand in the customary wave as I whizzed by the preoccupied recruits. A few kilometers later I was puzzled why I hadn't run into any traffic coming the other way, when suddenly as I was hugging the outside curve of the road, several chunks of rock cascaded down in front of me. I looked up to see more rocks falling from the cliff above. Then came the puzzling noises. Noises that sounded like muffled firecrackers followed by pinging sounds. As I rounded an S curve I noticed another group of Greek soldiers blocking off the road with their military vehicle. Frantically gesturing and waving their hands at me, the officer in charge sprinted towards me.

"What are you doing here?! Where did you come from? Didn't you see the road block four kilometers back?" he screamed.

Perplexed I replied, "There was no road block, just a bunch of soldiers relaxing and smoking under a tree."

"Look down there,' he gestured pointing to another group of soldiers in the ravine below the road, 'We're conducting target practice on this stretch of road; the road is closed for the next two hours."

"Well,' I countered, 'your comrades at the other end aren't aware of it and allowed me to proceed."

In a typical animated Greek manner, he explained that the noises I had heard ringing above my head were bullets ricocheting off the rocks. The soldiers, down in the ravine unable to see me, were shooting at targets a few meters above the very road I had just passed through.

Thinking to myself later that night Greek marksmen are either very, very good or very, very bad. The birthday was not the only reason for celebration that day.

SHOPPING IN IKARIA

The business district of Agios, the largest town on Ikaria, consists mostly of small shops run by individual proprietors always eager and willing to serve their hurried customers. Unfortunately, modern banking practices have yet to make major inroads with these small shop owners. When one buys an item it is best to have the exact amount as shop owners only keep a limited number of coins in their cash drawers. If change is to be given to a customer, quite often he or she might be given a small token or item in place of change. It is not unusual at the local pharmacy, for example, to be given one or two Band-Aids or several aspirins as change. I always love going to the pharmacy with great excitement and anticipation wondering what kind of change I'll get that day, maybe a couple of Ricola cough drops or a tablet or two of Vicodin.

One of my more puzzling purchases was made at a local hole-in-the-wall hardware stores. I was informed one day by my wife that a new outdoor clothesline was needed to replace the old flimsy and tattered one. She figured about fifteen meters was required. With this information fresh in my mind I hopped on my trusty Vespa and took off for Agios. As I popped into the first hardware store, I promptly spied a large spool of clothesline sitting right there on the counter. Thinking this was going to be a quick and easy transaction I confidently asked the saleslady for fifteen meters of line. She said nothing just looked at me mystified and bewildered. I thought to myself she did not understand me, so I repeated my utilitarian request for fifteen meters of line. Again, only to be met by more flustered looks.

Finally, I picked up the spool of line and once again said, "I need fifteen meters of this." Looking at me like I should know better she calmly explained,

"We only sell clothesline by the kilo." It took about a minute for me to fathom her reply. "You don't sell by the meter, only by the kilo?" I responded. "Yes, of course only by the kilo" came her curtsied reply. "Ok," I said "let me just measure out about fifteen meters of line then you can take it and weigh it on your scale, and charge me what it's worth." So, finally with a convergence of two scales of measurement I was able to purchase my fifteen meters of clothesline so our wet bathing suits and towels could hang and dry in the hot Greek sun.

CONTRADICTIONS

Contradictions are as numerous on Ikaria as cicadas in August. One of my favorite contradictions involves the law enforcement agency i.e. the Ikarian police, and their seemingly arbitrary and somewhat hazy enforcement of Greek motor vehicle laws. During my summers on Ikaria the run-ins I've had with the local police consisted mostly of minor motor vehicle violations. These so called violations always seemed to be selective or maybe they were somehow related to the phases of the moon, but nonetheless they happened and they should be duly noted with some kind of a plausible explanation. Those of us, who have bikes, on Ikaria everything from a Vespa to a Harley, are required by Greek law to wear a helmet, or at least have a helmet handy. When the police decide to enforce this law they will set up a road block for an hour or two, usually under the shade of a large tree and see who they can catch sans helmet. My three experiences with these police road blocks are quite varied and so are the results.

Experience #1
My first experience happened as I was riding my Vespa to Agios as usual without a helmet and unaware of a road block just outside the city limits. As I approached the police road block I purposely slowed down in anticipation of being stopped by the Ikarian police, but because both officers were busy with their official duties of writing tickets they motioned me to continue without stopping. How fortunate I thought, maybe my Vespa is too cute or too slow to warrant a warning or a ticket. So, my first experience reinforced in me a false sense of motor vehicle security.

Experience #2
Two years later, once again riding to Agios on my Vespa without a helmet, I encountered another police road block. Thinking I had free passage I whizzed past the blockade only to have an officer quickly chase me down and pull me over. Asking to see my driver's license, I searched my back pack only to

discover I had left my wallet with all my identification back at the house. Explaining the situation to the perturbed officer he allowed me twenty-four hours to present myself and my drivers' license, which happened to be a Michigan drivers' license, to the police station.

The next day being a bit fearful and uncertain of my status with the Ikarian police, I asked my good friend, Giovanni to accompany me to the police station in case some unexpected development occurred like being thrown in the Ikarian jail. He could thus relay the news of my imprisonment to my supportive wife. Upon reaching the police station and finding the main desk I explained to the duty officer the reason for my presence. "Fine," he said, "let's see your driver's license." Reaching into my back pocket I produced my wallet with all my identification cards. Fumbling to find my driver's license, my local Michigan library card happened to fall on the desk. The officer picked it up, examined it closely and asked, "Is this your driver's license?" Jokingly I replied, "Oh yeah." "Well, ok", he said shaking his head as if he didn't want to be bothered by such mundane civil infractions, "you're free to go." This thin piece of plastic had no identifying photograph, had no printed address, had no affiliation to the Michigan driver's bureau. The card did however have a cute graphic of two books leaning together and a helpful list of near-by branches. That magic combination was evidently all I needed. Hastily I picked up my get out of jail free card, tucked it safely in my wallet, thanked the kind officer and with a dazed and confused Giovanni made a swift exit out of the police station.

Experience #3
This latest encounter with the inglorious police road block occurred on a return trip to my village. By this time, I had acquired a helmet, or what would pass for a motorcycle helmet since it was really nothing more than one of those hard foam bicycle helmets. My son, Alex, was my passenger on the Vespa, and he unfortunately did not have a helmet. Spotting the road block about half a kilometer away, I quickly donned my fraudulent helmet, but then started worrying about my helmetless son. Stopping at the road block, the police officer approached and giving my improvised helmet a cursory glance, asked the usual to see my driver's license. After a quick glimpse at the license he waved us on. By this time my curiosity was inflamed. "Excuse me," I asked, "is everyone on a motorcycle supposed to wear a helmet?" "No," he replied, "just the driver, passengers aren't required to wear helmets." As we motored back to our village I couldn't help but wonder if this was the same panel of Solon lawmakers that also made the no smoking law for the bank customers, but not for the bank employees.

WHAT A DAY (A MYTH)

It was one of those perfectly unblemished summer days that we freely imagine and wistfully long for, when the mountain winds caress the warm, sunbaked rocks on a quiet beach. There, gently rolling in, are the waves rising from the dark, cerulean sea tumbling upon the receptive shore. Then the rocks, the rocks that have stood eons as a garrison lining the shore, having withstood both tempest winds and crashing waves, provide a respite for weary wayfarers.

It was during this perfect summer day the three major players the wind, the rocks, and the waves, each gave testimony as to why their presence made it so. The wind, huffing and puffing, and always in a hurry, spoke up first, "It seems to me, that to have such a day, my wind needs to be at a certain speed and with just the right amount of force. Otherwise there would be no gently lapping waves, and with too much wind it would produce a blustery day."

"Well, your winds might blow both strong and weak," replied the rocks in a tarry voice, "but we are the ones, large and small that deflect and direct the winds around this beach. We offer shade and protection from the gust. Without us, there would be no perfect summer day."

Finally, the waves in a rumbling voice spoke up, "You both have good points about your contributions for such a splendid summer day, but don't forget, it is the force of the waves that can move you, rocks all around this beach. It is I, who really generates the perfect summer day." With that, all three dramatists once again, resumed claiming credit with slightly elevated voices as to who makes the perfect summer beach day.

As this cacophony continued, a faint and distant voice could be heard. A fatigued human voice, pleading for help far out on the wide-spread horizon, was noticed first by the perceptive waves. The wind, also sensing danger, alertly looked around and immediately detected a tiny fishing boat. The fisherman waving his arms in desperation, was floundering in the sea. Rushing to the boat, the wind saw it was in disrepair and full of smoke.

Calling upon his companion the waves, together they cautiously escorted the speck of a fishing vessel towards the shore, where the rocks were waiting for the boats' arrival. Seeing the shore quickly approaching, the fisherman made ready to disembark. He flung his line over the nearest large rock and secured the boat to the boulder. Scrambling to shore the exhausted fisherman looked up at the wind, over at the waves, and leaned feebly against a rock.

He cocked his head back and was heard to say in a crackling voice, "Thank you, if it wasn't for you waves who first saw me, and you wind who helped steer my boat to shore, and you rocks who secured my boat, it would only have been a matter of time before I would have perished on the open sea. I know that the three of you working together saved my life, thank you, thank you, thank you," said the grateful fisherman.

In a flash of realization, the wind acknowledged that just as the three elements collaborated together to rescue the man they also together create, the optimal beach day.

"If one of us is missing, then there is no perfect day," chimed in the waves.

"We are all important and play a role," said the rocks.

So, next time you are outdoors to appreciate such an occurrence, know it is nature working all her elements in harmony resulting in those perfect summer days.

TRAVELS WITH DAD PART I

It's not often a son gets a chance to travel exclusively with his father to some far flung exotic destination. Usually family, time and economic restraints limit such rare partnerships. During the summer of 1989, I had the opportunity to take such an excursion with my father to a remote and distant Greek island called Ikaria. The island where my father was born and raised, and where I also spent my first five years of life. The purpose of this father and son journey was the building of a family summer home. Naively, I thought this four week stay on Ikaria would be a combination of work and play. Laboring arduously in the mornings with the builders and then spending the hot afternoons lying on the pebble beaches under the sea pines with the warm Aegean breezes blowing over my body. Such were my idealistic and visionary vacation dreams.

Wanderlust was an inherent part of my father's personality. He had traveled extensively during World War II, and continued somewhat after the war. He was always ready and able at the drop of a hat to grab his passport and head to his Aegean island home. He was a man slight in stature, full head of grey hair, bi-spectacled with a thin 1940's style mustache, and always full of energy and on the move. My father had the distinction, or maybe I should say a "devil's mark" when it came to traveling. He always seemed to bring about some unpredictable, chaotic and challenging misadventure, which usually required others to come to his rescue and bail him out of his predicament at the last moment. It's not that he went looking for such misadventures, they just naturally happen to occurred around him. This would include any ordinary, mundane exposure to the outside world, whether a trip to the local grocery store, or a trip half way around the world.

My journey started innocently enough when I kissed and said farewell to my wife, my seven-year-old son and my six-month old daughter. Jokingly I mentioned to my wife, it would be a highly successful trip if both my father and I returned unscathed and alive from Greece. My curt comment referred to the fact, as it was widely known by all, that my father's magnetism for misadventure grated and infuriated me to no end. I figured occupying my father's time with full days of work on the house should keep him out of harm's way, and away from any embarrassing mischief.

Our trek started peacefully enough on a Sabena flight out of Chicago to Athens, with a stop in Brussels. Events quickly took a dark and ominous turn as we left Brussels, when almost immediately we hit a thunderstorm of massive proportions over Belgium. A storm so immense we couldn't fly over it or around it. Then when the pilot came on the intercom in a stern Gaelic voice and announced that dinner would not be served because of the turbulence, and for the stewardess to strap in, we knew instinctively we would be in for quite a ride. During the next two and a half hours every disposable sick bag and container on board was put to good use as the plane lurched violently from side to side, sometimes seemly dropping several hundred feet at a time in elevation. The plane fuselage was filled with the sporadic screams of mothers, the moans of grown men and the crying of young babies, along with the varied and countless prayers offered to the Gods by the nervous and apprehensive passengers. Even my father being a relative stoic figure, mumbled and swore under his breath using words that I had never heard before. Finally, as we approached Athens the storm eased, and we all took reconnaissance of our sore and aching bodies, passing the bags and containers down to the stewardess who profusely apologized for the lack of our in-flight meal.

Thinking that the worse part of our trip was over, and glad to be on solid ground, we gallantly, still on wobbly legs and queasy stomachs from the jarring plane ride went trooping up to the passport control window only to come face to face with the notoriously ubiquitous Greek bureaucracy. My father in his younger and more idealistic years happened to be a Communist sympathizer and after World War II was briefly detained by the Allies in an army detainee camp in Egypt for expressing his radical views. As we handed our American passports to the passport official he immediately pulled out what seemed to be a rather large size 20 shoe box, full of 5x7 note cards. When he came to the M's he pulled out a card with my dad's last name on it, along with a brief dossier. Looking suspiciously at my father then intently studying his card, the official made a comment in regards, that my father, now an American citizen, must have accepted the glories of capitalism and the proper and correct political views, and thus would be allowed to enter Greece. I, on the other hand knew better, and before my father had a chance to open his mouth to express what he really thought were the correct political views, I grabbed him by the arm, thanked the passport official and briskly pushed my dad through the turnstile and proceeded to drag him to the baggage area muttering something about capitalist pigs, or maybe he was channeling Karl Marx.

Having survived the passport ordeal and now firmly planted on Greek soil, like a true Odysseus longing to get home, we moved to the next challenging task of collecting our luggage. Luckily our suitcases were already on the baggage carousel, a feat which I believe was, and possibly still is a world record time for Greek airport baggage handlers. As I lifted my dad's suitcase off the conveyer I became suspicious of its' enormous weight.

I turned and asked him, "Why does your suitcase weigh so much?"

He swiftly answered, "I just have a few things for the house and my clothes, come on let's go."

Our final stop in exiting the airport was customs. Normally, the Greek custom officials don't want to be bothered with the task of ordering tourists to open their suitcases and having to pilfer through all their soiled clothing and belongings. They usually give you a summary glance and wave you through. As we hastily passed the first group of custom officials one of them, who looked like a heavy from an old black and white T.V. Western, unexpectedly started to glare at us, as if we were mentally suspect. Stepping around the other officials he approached us and asked if we had anything to declare.

My father in his rush to exit the airport quickly chirped in, "No, no we have nothing to declare, we're fine, nothing to declare, our suitcases are all right," words that seemed to resonate off the building walls, and which immediately raised the suspicion of the less than sympathetic custom agent. Commanding his most surly voice and with a cigarette dangling loosely from his lips the official with his head held high ordered us to follow him.

"There," he pointed, to a large steel table, "put your luggage there, and open them up. Let's see what you don't have to declare" he said in an officious manner.

Now my father, reflecting back on his knowledge of functionaries and people in positions that could possibly be influenced to ignore breaches of rules and guidelines, had packed inside his suitcase, what he considered to be the international symbol of bribery, cigarettes. Not just any cigarettes, but the most revered, coveted and preferred brand in the world, Marlboro Reds. Immediately my father fumbled around, opened his large and heavy suitcase and there on top were two sealed cartons of Marlboro Reds. Glancing at the customs agent, my father cunningly smiled and giving him a wink or two, stood quietly by waiting for the official to confiscate the two prized cartons for his personal enjoyment. Unfortunately, this scene was played out in an open public area with other officials watching this comical scenario closely. The customs official, feeling the glare of a dozen eyes on him promptly ignored the cigarette payola and started his dutiful search of the suitcase. Reaching to the bottom of the suitcase, while giving my father a curious and perplexed look, he pulled out an old, beat-up framing hammer.

My father instantly pleaded, "That's my favorite hammer, and I need it to build my house."

In a calm and collected voice the official replied, "We have hammers in Greece, in fact we've had hammers for thousands of years." Dropping the American made hammer back in the suitcase, he once again reached his hand in the pile of my dad's clothing and this time emerged with a hack saw and a half dozen replacement blades. By now I was totally speechless and just as mystified as the customs agent. I had no idea my father was carrying such unconventional travel items, I imagined the next tool to be unearthed was going to be a Paul Bunyan type ax. Examining the saw and the blades, the official shaking his head in a bewildered manner, threw them casually back in the suitcase toolbox.

"Open the rest of your bags" he ordered. Nimbly we proceeded to open the remaining three suitcases, wondering how much longer this inquisition was going to continue. Apparently by now the official was also becoming frustrated, seeing that we really didn't have any meaningful contraband to speak of just a rag tag collection of old tools.

He gave our bags a quick once over then abruptly said, "Close them, you can go." In a flash the suitcases were slammed shut, still containing the two not so enticing cartons of Marlboro Reds and with passports hot in hand we briskly walked out of the airport and headed to the taxi stand.

Commandeering the first taxi we could find, we slung our suitcases in the trunk, gave the driver the address of our hotel, and settled in the backseat of the taxi for the half hour car ride. It was at this point I realized I could finally relax after the non-stop events of the past few hours, which had seemed to have lingered for days. Jet lag had caught up with me as the taxi maneuvered cautiously in and out of traffic, and just when my eyes shut for a quick cat nap we arrived at our hotel. Sluggishly we crawled out of the taxi, retrieved our suitcases, and paid the cab driver, who courteously wished us a restful and peaceful vacation.

Approaching the hotel entrance with our luggage in hand, my father looked around and in a soft voice said, "I think I left my jacket in the back seat of the cab."

"Don't worry," I said, "we'll buy a new one tomorrow."
In an even softer voice he whispered "My passport is in my jacket."

"What?!" I exploded, "Your passport?!" Without a moment's hesitation I dropped my suitcases, looked around and then down the narrow street I spotted our taxi, two blocks away, stuck in mid-afternoon traffic. I took off running at a speed that still amazes me to this day, hoping that the taxi would remain locked in the everlasting traffic jam. About half a block away I saw the stalled taxi starting to move and pick up momentum as it approached a major intersection. Thinking I had no hope of catching up to the cab, I immediately started to orchestrate in my mind the dreaded and time consuming trip to the U.S. embassy, and the explanation I would have to give the embassy official. Could my father's personality suffice as an explanation?

Suddenly with what seemed like divine intervention, as the cab sped up to cross the busy street, the traffic light turned red. With an unusual squeal of the brakes the cab abruptly stopped at the crosswalk just in time for me to catch up to it. Winded and out of breath, I banged on the taxi window shocking the startled driver, who instinctively thought he was going to be robbed by a hot sweaty, mad man. It took me a minute to catch my breath and through heavy breathing I explained that my dad's jacket was somewhere in the cab. The driver unaware of the mislaid garment and its' contents, looked around and on the back floor found the jacket scrunched under the seat. Handing me the wayward jacket, passport still snugly secured in the inside pocket, accompanied by my father's wallet, with all his money I thanked the stunned cabbie.

Holding my dad's jacket, as one holds a holy book, I lethargically walked back to the hotel. The hot afternoon sun, jet lag, an empty stomach, combined with the unexpected jolt of physical activity turned my mind into a congealed glob of mush. I was left with one sobering thought, it had only been a few hours since my father and I started this exhausting journey, what else could possibly happen to us in the next few weeks? I reached the entrance of the hotel to find my father sitting on a stool silently waiting for me. I presented him the jacket and without saying a word we both turned and entered the hotel lobby knowing this father and son odyssey was just commencing.

Maybe Zorba the Greek was right, when he said, "Life is trouble, death is not, to be alive is to undo your belt and look for trouble." My father not only removed his belt, but his jacket, shoes and socks as well. I realized that the next four weeks, would be not only challenging in trying to keep my father safe and out of trouble, but a trial of my capacity for endurance, patience and civility. All these attributes were going to be inevitably and severely tested in the days to come when we reached Ikaria.

TRAVELS WITH DAD PART II

Most Greeks when faced with a major construction project, will use whatever money they have available, proceed to purchase what materials they can afford, and start the lengthy building process. When the money runs out construction comes to a complete halt. Workers are dismissed and what piles of materials, stone, sand, bricks, etc. remain are just left there waiting for the next injection of money. This prolonged period of time could last weeks, months or even years before construction can once a gain resume.

This start and stop construction cycle with its' various mounds of materials scattered all over the Greek countryside was a particular annoyance to my father's convoluted sense of organization and order. When we finally arrived on Ikaria, after our arduous beginnings, some of the building materials we ordered, primarily the bricks, were already delivered. These pavers were brought by a dilapidated dump truck that casually and not too carefully unloaded them in our front yard establishing an enormous sienna colored pile of bricks, instantly creating condos for countless families of scorpions and lizards. Immediately my father seeing this vast and seemingly endless pile of bricks began a verbal assault on the Greek truck drivers for their inconsiderate and lackadaisical care given to his precious and cherished building materials.

My dad and I, tired from our long and exhausting trip, turned in early that first night hoping to get some much needed sleep. Sometime during the night or early morning hours, a strange and mysterious sound coming from the darken yard kept reverberating in my ears. A sound vaguely similar to a young child knocking together his play toys in a consistent and rhythmic pattern.

Knowing that no child would be up at this ungodly time of night, I crawled out of bed and made my way to the window. There, as dawn was breaking over the eastern tip of Ikaria, was my father in his scruffy work clothes care fully arranging the scattered bricks in neat and orderly rows, like soldiers in formation waiting for their marching orders.

"What are you doing?" I yelled in a parched voice. "You know it's barely five o clock in the morning, people are trying to sleep!" My bellowing had no noticeable effect on my zombie like dad. He just kept on methodically arranging his brick army in readiness for their battle with the bricklayers later on that day. In desperation I quickly slipped on my sandals ran out of the house towards my father, just in time to see him place the last brick, like a royal coronation, on top of the last row. Grabbing him by the arm as one grabs a mischievous child, I shouted at him. "You can't be doing this in the middle of the night, everyone and everything neighbors, dogs, mules, goats are trying to sleep and you should too." Grumpy and exhausted, but tepid from his nocturnal employment, I led him back to the house, as he explained to me that bricks have to be properly and systematically arranged in order for the bricklayers to work under optimal conditions. Finally, as the first rooster was heard across the hollow and the eastern sky turned crimson red my father went to sleep.

With typical haphazard of starts and stops the building of the additional bedroom began in earnest. Among the many and inconvenient distractions to the process was surprisingly, the elderly village priest, who presided over not one but three churches in our small village. One of the churches, affectionately known as Number Two, was situated right below and adjacent to our property. Given the location and the general direction of the summer winds, the church yard, as well as the church itself, was often encrusted in layers of blowing sand, dust, and cement powder from our ever expanding construction site.

The rakish priest, a late septuagenarian, was a contemporary of my father, both having grown up on the island and having a long history of personal skirmishes and disputes. None the less, every day he climbed the fourteen stairs from the church yard up to our house, enjoyed the customary glass of ouzo, and shared with my father the latest village gossip. This daily routine lasted about an hour, an hour that my father felt was useless and wasted on the priest, because it took precious time away from his work and the overseeing of the workers. He made his views known in a hushed voice every day when the priest was descending the fourteen stairs to the church yard below.

As construction continued and the meltimi winds picked up, the priest in his daily visits would complain to my father of the debris and mess created around the church. In response my father in his most diplomatic voice, would deflect the priest's complaints, and state that he had no personal command over Mother Nature and her relentless winds. Ultimately, these too frequent bouts of grievances came to a head one bright gusty morning.

The priest was once again sweeping the construction sand and dust out of the church entrance, when in a fit of total exasperation stopped sweeping and called up to my father, "Come see what mayhem your workers and the wind have created inside this house of God." On this day my father must have had on his cranky pants and was in no mood to take verbal abuse from this man of God. As the barrage of words escalated between the two septuagenarians, the workers hearing the torrent of threats and retribution sensed that something inconceivable might happen.

Then, in what appeared to be a split second the wind stopped, the cicadas became silent, the workers dropped their tools, and in unison watched this geriatric smack down unfold. My father in the heat of the moment, promptly picked up a nearby shovel, and lacing the morning air with a slew of obscenities raced down the stairs. He ceased only momentarily to graphically describe how he was going to grab and pull the scraggily beard of the priest, twist and squeeze it like a pretzel around his scrawny neck, so he no longer would have to listen to the daily bitching of the holy man. The priest, alarmed at the sudden appearance of his half-crazed neighbor, stood defiantly in the church entrance, head held high, clutching and holding out the gold Orthodox cross hanging from his neck. My father, still seeing red, instinctively swung his improvised weapon wildly in a dervish manner high above his head.

Suddenly, with a thundering clamor, he brought it belligerently down at the feet of the startled priest, still embracing his protective cross, and scattering the accumulated piles of sand and debris. The two combatants now sweating and exhausted by their morning joust, stood silently, glaring eye to eye and heaving laboriously, as two depleted heavyweights.

Swiftly, I flew down the stairs and placed myself between the two warriors trying to interject an air of tranquility, but I was irrelevant for the remainder of the event. As the level of adrenaline slowly decreased in the two bellicose neighbors, a shred of calm appeared in their behaviors. They had taken their positions to the limit, and finally acknowledged the futility of their actions.

Only with the last batch of cement mixed and the last brick laid in place, would this daily skirmish cease. This realization was understood by both of them, and with a grandiose gesture my father assured the priest, that when construction was finally completed, he himself would come down and personally clean the church and the church yard. This confrontation was the talk of the village for months, and each time the story was told it embellished and elevated the personas of the two combatants, casting them as the clash of the two septuagenarian titans.

TRAVELS WITH DAD PART III

Neighbors quickly recognized the quirkiness of my father's behaviors and as village gossip spread like locust in August about the peculiar habits of my father, a clever prank was hatched by our amicable neighbor, Christos. He was a rather provocative catalyst, a speculator in a way, always looking for a semi-shady financial deal to make him rich. His personality was effervescent and disarming, just the right mix that attracted my dad to him. Christos and my father immediately became comrades in arms, and provided additional fodder for the villagers as the two companions seemed to terrorize half of Ikaria with their exuberant wisecracks and antics.

The closed ranks of the brick army were being diminished swiftly by the bricklayers, as the bedroom progressed. Eventually a pile numbering about two hundred remained intact for the final push and completion of the bedroom. By now, my father's sleeping pattern had once again changed. Helping out the workers during the day by hauling bricks, mixing cement and running errands exhausted him physically and by 10:00 p.m. he was in his bed sound asleep.

Throughout this tumultuous building process our inquisitive neighbor Christos made daily reconnaissance to observe and record the progress of the bricklayers, all the while quaffing a glass or two of ouzo with my dad and joking about his natural affinity with the bricks. The aggregate of these scouting visits was the formation of a deviously ingenious joke, at the expense of my father. It was a short time later during a hot and windy night that Christos stealthily made his way to the last remaining battalion of bricks, still precariously occupying a corner of our yard. Within two hours he had singlehandedly transported my dad's precious stash to his side yard, a mere twenty meters from our house, and covered it with a large green tarp. Christos' fiendish klepto plan was basically to enjoy my father's baffled and confused look in finding his famously proprietary bricks had somehow mysteriously vanished in thin air. He moved his rickety table and chair to the edge of his porch so as to embrace the best view of my father's emergence from the house and the bewilderment to follow. The morning sun had already cleared the horizon as my father stepped out of the house to inspect the previous day's work, when he stopped in his tracks. Perplexed by the sight of the missing bricks, he promptly assumed the actions of a possessed man. Words flew out of his mouth like machine gun fire.

"My bricks, my bricks, someone stole my bricks, they're gone, the bricks, the bricks!" He ran from the yard to the church below desperately seeking some kind of divine intervention on his behalf, while filling the sky with stinging blasphemies. His agonizing pursuit continued onto the main street, still in a frenzy yelling "My bricks, my bricks, my bricks!" dashing wildly throughout the neighborhood and once again waking up the confused and groggy villagers.

All the while our rascally neighbor was watching him from his porch chuckling at the amusing antics of my father's painful search for his bricks. Finally, when Christos could no longer contain himself with all this merriment, he called to my father to check out the suspiciously tarp covered pile. My father swiftly raced the twenty meters to Christos' side yard, pulled back the green tarp to expose his precious collection of sienna colored bricks. A combination of relief, anger and amusement enveloped my father, luckily the amused part won out, as he shook his head slowly and a smile crossed his face, he realized the joke was on him. As morning coffee was shared by the two companionable neighbors the account of the missing bricks escapade was repeated numerous times, and laughter filled the quiet morning air.

Eventually the additional bedroom was completed, but that did not end the saga of my father and the neighborhood jokester. The summer passed quickly for me and I had to return to the States, but my father remained an additional three weeks to tie up loose ends with the workers and the bureaucratic Greek building codes. It was on the last day of my dad's extended stay on Ikaria that Christos came by to say good-bye and to wish my hurried father a safe journey back to Chicago. He presented my dad a package the size of a carton of cigarettes, nicely wrapped with a colorful ribbon and bow.

The package was meant for a mutual friend, Anna, who was going to meet my father at O'Hare airport. The contents of the package Christos declared were prescription drugs for this friend, drugs that were much cheaper in Greece, thanks to socialized medicine, than in the States. Not to be derelict towards a friend in need, my father unabashedly agreed to transport this needed medication. Since my father had already packed his antiquated suitcase to the gills, he was forced to re-pack leaving several small gifts behind, to accommodate this hefty medical parcel.

The return trip for my father was a slow and gruesome one, most appropriate for travelers to and from Greece at that time. The ferry from Ikaria to

Piraeus was six hours late, his stay in Athens had to be extended by two days, and his Sabena flight back to Chicago arrived hours behind schedule. Throughout all these delays and constrains he carefully and meticulously guarded his luggage with the medicine safely secured, tucked in the inside compartment of his suitcase.

Finally, arriving at O'Hare and uncommonly breezing through customs, he was met by the anxious Anna. Immediately my father opened his venerable suitcase and judiciously pulled out her brightly wrapped gift.
Perplexed by this magnanimous gesture on the part of my father, she asked "What is it?"

"It's the medicine you asked Christos to send you from Greece" he replied.

"I never asked him to send me any meds' she countered, somewhat confused 'but let's see what it is." Deftly she removed the bright ribbon and tore into the wrapping paper. Their world, in the middle of O'Hare airport, seemed to stand still as they tried to focus their eyes on the heavy object gently resting in Anna's trembling hand. What my father had so painstakingly and vigilantly escorted for days, across two continents and over five thousand miles, was one of his brick soldiers, regulation-sized, sienna colored brick, compliments of good neighbor Christos.

The trip was put in proper perspective a few years later after my father passed away, the excursion we took together was the last one he took to his beloved Ikaria. It was only then that I was able to appreciate those periods of daily mayhem that included arguments and squabbles with the locals, as with the cantankerous old priest, overdue or inebriated workers, and annoying but amusing neighbors. In the end we both survived, returned home with various bumps and bruises and plenty of emotional scars that are the transitional outcomes of such father and son expeditions. Chronicling this story, I'm left with the visionary words of the poet Anne Sexton, 'It doesn't matter who my father was, it matters who I remember he was."

THE NEW AIRPORT

Typically, islands rely on harbors for transportation, it is not often an airport is built, and in the case of Ikaria it wasn't until the late 90's. The airport, at the time was one long continuous airstrip with no building or tower. To make it long enough for planes to land, tons of rock and dirt were moved and deposited on the eastern tip of Ikaria where unlike the rest of the island, the land is semi-flat. Actually, the rocks and dirt were dumped off the coast into the Aegean so the runway could be of adequate length. The fact that the airstrip was located in an area of sparse population did not stop the Ikarians from making pilgrimages to the site to offer their comments on the progress of the airport, or to provide their own highly knowledgeable opinions on which direction the runway should be built.

As the last of the concrete was being poured for the runway, I received a rather unusual travel request. It seemed that my caretaker's daughter-in-law, Irene, had always wanted to learn how to drive a manual automobile. The only vehicle available was an old, lumbering, rusted out 1974 VW cargo van. A van that had traversed the main roads, back roads and goat trails of Ikaria for over twenty-five faithful years. It was in this vehicle she hoped to learn the intricacies of clutching, down shifting and the ever elusive reverse. The only area accessible and available for such instruction of course, was the newly built airport runway. The date of our first driving lesson was set, a late summer afternoon. As I was preparing for my first drive out to the airstrip, I was politely informed that several of the village dignitaries wished to accompany us on this adventurous driving lesson. This was a golden opportunity for them to view this modern day aeronautical marvel.

The VW van could normally seat three adults comfortably in the front. The back of the van was empty so that farm implements, animal feed or animals could be easily transported. In no time the number of passengers quickly climbed to a dozen. With typical Ikarian ingenuity, benches, lawn chairs and stools were summoned and attached with sturdy ropes to the inside panels of the van to provide seating for the entourage. The ride to the airport was rather like a large family going on a picnic, stories were told, jokes were shared and laughter filled the van on our forty-five-minute ride. Upon our arrival the talking and laughing suddenly seized as I parked the van at one end of the runway. A look of utter amazement, somewhat like a spiritual awakening, overtook the passengers as they gazed out over the immense and seemingly endless concrete field.

I instructed the dazed travelers to disembark so I could begin the first driving lesson. The lesson primarily consisted of teaching my protégé how to clutch, shift, find the correct gear, and apply the gas and to brake. As Irene took the sputtering van from one end of the runway to the other, she would wave joyously to the assembled entourage as we lurched and squealed past them. Like a homecoming queen in a parade, she greeted the crowd whose eyes were glued to her. The driving lesson lasted for six jarring trips, from one end of the runway to the other. The now confident student driver had had enough of cruising back and forth for her audience and was ready to head home.

The trip back to the village consisted of two main topics, the glory and honor that was going to be the airport of Ikaria, and the impressive driving skills of the novice driver. True to the family outing form, we concluded the festive trip with a stop at the nearest kafenion to toast the new driver and her courageous accomplishments.

FLYING TO IKARIA

Flying to Ikaria is a relatively short trip, about half an hour or so from Athens. The modest twin engine turbo-prop flies in low, lands, drops off its' passengers, picks up another group of passengers and returns to the mainland. Such is the normal mundane routine of flying in and out of Ikaria, or so it seemed when my wife and I escorted our son to the airport for his flight back to Athens. The Olympic Airlines plane arrived on time, that is Greek time, about twenty minutes late. The passengers disembarked full of laughter with the anticipation of spending time on this idyllic Aegean island. The departing passengers slowly made their way through passport control, then security clearance and trudged out to the tarmac to board the vintage plane. Once the travelers boarded the plane, the airport staff seemed to disappear most likely to go out to lunch, take an afternoon nap or hit the beaches.

This time my wife and I decided to stay and watch the plane carrying our son take off. Since the airport only has one runway, the plane must turn around, taxi down to one end hidden behind a hill, rev up its' engines, race down the runway and take off. Several long minutes went by as we patiently stood under the hot Aegean sun waiting for the plane to emerge from behind the hill, when suddenly all sorts of sirens went off. Out of the airport two firemen came dashing out, boarded their fire truck with lights flashing and sirens whining, they made a beeline towards the plane. Immediately confusion, fear and a troubling sensation shook my body. Running back into the airport to ask what is going on, I found it deserted! The only person still around was the cashier at a small café cleaning tables. Anxiously I approached her about the ominous excursion of the fire truck.

"Oh, that," she replied, "the fire truck is chasing the goats off the runway so the plane can take off, it happens quite often." Relieved that our son's plane was not on fire, but rather under siege by Ikarian goats, I relayed the bizarre news to my worried wife.

Ikaria, it seems, has a sizable number of wild goats that roam and graze in the mountains above the airport, and often meander down to the airstrip looking for a morsel or two. Their omnivorous habits endanger the plane during its' arrivals and departures. So, if you are fortunate enough to fly in or out of Ikaria, look out your window and you might see those hungry Ikarian goats scavenging around the airfield looking for that last morsel of food. If you are luckier yet, you may see the fire truck cruising down the runway scaring off the hazardous goats.

THE ONE EURO STORE

Change is never easy especially in Ikaria. One of the most dramatic changes on the island happened when Greece converted from the drachma to the Euro in 2002. The Greek drachma up until 2002 was the oldest continuously used currency in the world.

Nowhere was the currency confusion more evident than in our little kafenion. The kindly owner, Aryiro, always seemed to have a difficult time in managing the small restaurant on her own, sometimes forgetting items that were ordered. The one area she seemed most perplexed in was figuring out a customer's change. With the introduction of the Euro her confusion turned into a full blown nightmare. In trying to convert drachmas to Euros, she spent more time doing the math than filling the pressing orders of her other customers. Food to be served was left on tables while she pounded away at her calculator over and over again. More often than not, exasperated customers would request a pad of paper and figure out the total bill themselves.

Not to let this condition of perpetual uncertainty linger much longer she came up with the perfect pricing scheme. Every item in her kafenion would become one Euro, from a cup of coffee, to an ice cream, to an ouzo to the meze, everything would be one Euro. A simple effective stress reducer that made her life and the lives of her customers easier, she became the first Ikarian One Euro Store.

WHERE'S THE MONEY FROM?

International money conspiracies, real or imaginary, seem to pop up on a regular basis like wild fires in the mountains of Ikaria. A recently uncovered banking ploy involves the rise of the new affluent Russians and their attempts to money launder their Rubles, Euros and U.S. dollars primarily in Cyprus and in Greece. Getting money out of Russia seems to be an ongoing and lucrative activity since the time of the Russian Czars. Wealthy Russians noting the somewhat lax banking laws and regulations in Greece and in Cyprus have established both real and bogus accounts in both countries. It has been rumored, and there is some credence to this rumor from the U.S. Treasury department, that there are more U.S. counterfeit one hundred dollar bills circulating in Russia than anywhere else in the world. This rumor certainly hasn't escaped notice with our provincial banking institutions on Ikaria.

Arriving in Ikaria from the States during the summer of 2012, with a handful of one hundred dollar bills fresh from Chase bank, I was anxious to exchange them for Euros before the inevitable summer swoon of the dollar against the Euro occurred. Clutching dearly on to my American passport I entered the diminutive, but highly air-conditioned Alpha Bank at Agios Kirikos, capital of Ikaria. I looked around somewhat warily and noticed there was little customer traffic in the bank, so I confidently figured this was going to be an easy in easy out banking transaction. Then I quickly recalled past banking experiences and remembered, not too fondly, there is no such thing as easy in easy out in Ikaria.

Immediately, as I handed the teller my freshly minted hundred dollar bills, she looked up at me with a suspicious glare undoubtedly trying to figure out what ruse I was trying to perpetrate. To ease the situation, I promptly produced my American passport which she grabbed with both hands and proceeded to closely examine the outside cover. Once satisfied, she opened it to the identification page glancing at my prison mug shot type photo, then at me during what seemed to be several uneasy moments. Finally, she picked up the hundred dollar bills, rubbed each one gently between her thumb and forefinger, then she held each one up to the light examining them all for any tell-tale sign that they might be counterfeit. Suddenly, with one harried scoop she picked up the bills along with my passport, stood up, turned and walked to a copy machine situated at the back of the bank. In no time she Zeroxed the main pages of my passport along with both sides of the one hundred dollar bills. Returning nonchalantly to her desk she proceeded to copy down by hand all the serial numbers of the bills onto the official exchange form. Giving me a copy of the form, she then stapled all the Zeroxed pages to the exchange document and filed them away, along with the hundred dollar bills in a large coffee stained manila folder. Seeing the muddled expression on my face she calmly reassured me, "We have to do this because of all the fake hundred dollar bills coming out of Russia." Nodding my head with approval I understood the ramifications to a small bank on Ikaria if it was to get stuck with a manila folder full of counterfeit one hundred dollar bills.

So, thanks to this new crop of Russian counterfeiters, next time I try to exchange my American dollars who knows what the bank might require for such a transaction, fingerprints, eye scans, signed affidavits, oaths of perpetual truthfulness, my computer passwords? The answer seems to be ditch the U.S. hundred dollar bills and enter the 21st century by just carrying an ATM card, but this being Ikaria I am left wondering what are the chances that any one of the four ATM machines on Ikaria might be working on the day I need one?

SALES SLIPS AND TAXES

Taxes (φ ό ρ ο υ ς) is probably the most feared word in the Greek language. Greeks historically have had an aversion to paying any kind of tax, for whatever purpose, and have gone to great lengths in avoiding them. With the economic depression still going on (as this is 2012), the current Greek government in its ongoing efforts to raise revenues, not only tightened tax laws, but also introduced a plethora of new taxes to be imposed on the population. This has led the Greeks to believe that the last several elected governments have been nothing more than a kleptocracy rather than a democracy, each one more corrupt than the last, bolstered by years of cronyism.

With the introduction of the new income tax came new challenges for the Greek taxpayer in trying to circumvent this hated legislation. According to the new tax a deduction would be given based on the kinds and amount of sales receipts one has accumulated during the year. Consequently, taxes are reduced correspondingly based on the tax bracket one finds himself in. So, throughout the year everyone is squirreling away sales receipts from a few Euro cents to mega Euro purchases. This has led to intriguing phenomena in which people are trading sales slips, as I remember trading baseball cards as a kid. "I'll give you two of my apparel receipts for one of your gas receipts." Or if a relative hasn't reached his or her maximum deductions, other family members may pitch in and donate some of their sales slips. What you can find in every household is a large shoe box brimming full of sales receipts that have to be kept for a year. If one has an accountant, then he has to safely store these receipts for all his clients.

During the summer of 2012, as we started a huge kitchen renovation project, I too started to accumulate large quantities of sales slips that I consciously hoarded in a size 44 shoe box. Then it occurred to me, since sales receipts were such a valuable commodity and in high demand, maybe I could make some extra money and auction them to the highest bidder. It was a fleeting thought, because I knew deep inside I would just give them away. Sure enough, by the end of the summer my niece wound up with my size 44 shoe box packed full of sales receipts, everything from a bag of pistachios to a new kitchen sink. So, maybe this just proves what the arch conservative, Barry Goldwater once said about income taxes, "The income tax created more criminals than any other single act of government."

THE LOTTERY

Ikaria has always been considered by other Greeks as an island outpost, somewhat backwards and full of loveable but eccentric locals. Ikarians certainly do not see themselves described in such unflattering and uncouth terms. They see themselves rather as proud, independent and creative individuals. The creative theme struck a chord with me one day in Agios. While returning to my car I was hastily approached by one of our amiable local farmers. This particular farmer decided a few years ago to relocate to a miniscule trailer that he set up in a middle of a deep ravine, a ravine that during the rainy winter months would cascade tons of rainwater down to the Aegean. Nevertheless, he settled into this risky nook amidst the boulders, cacti and the torrential rains. He was even able to somehow gather and herd several farm animals around his little trailer.

As this whimsical and robust stranger approached me I spotted him holding in one hand a gigantic roll of paper. At first I thought it was a roll of industrial size toilet paper, and this was one of those bodily function emergencies, but as I looked closer I realized it was a large roll of register tape. He quickly cornered me and dove into his animated scheme describing how I could win his highly prized mule in a lottery he was conducting. The cost of a lottery ticket was a mere Euro. It turned out he had written double numbers on the roll of register tape, and as a contestant purchased a number he would tear off the duplicate number and deposit it in his goat skin sack along with the other purchased numbers. Eventually when he figured he had sold a sufficient number of tickets to make a handsome profit on his prized mule, he would draw the winning number from his sack.

Realizing that this was the only way I would ever be a mule owner, and not thinking of the consequences and responsibilities of owning the animal, I immediately bought five tickets. Driving home that afternoon in a justifiable daze with the five tickets tucked in my pocket, I was seeing myself naming my mule some kind of studly name, and picturing myself triumphantly galloping into Agios on the back of my speedy hybrid. A couple of weeks later

I found myself one evening at our local kafenion, when suddenly I thought of the lottery. Curiously I asked around if anyone heard who won the mule sweepstakes. "The old farmer drew a number just a few days ago," said one of the regulars, "A cousin of his won." In one quick blow, my dreams of being a mule driver crashed but I smiled thinking about how many others had also invested their Euros in this lucrative mule lottery.

THE LADY BUYS A WEAPON

Enter any small Ikarian grocery store, the kind that resembles a glorified hole in the wall, and you will find surprisingly large variety of food and non- food items. Among the fresh fruit and vegetables you will find shelves crammed from ceiling to floor with a vast collection of canned, wrapped and boxed items, and usually one or two articles that will leave you scratching your head as to "what is this?" The day I went shopping at my favorite grocery store in Agios Kirikos turned out to be a busy shopping day for locals. I found myself impatiently waiting in the check-out line behind a rather plump but pleasant elderly woman, buying her daily goods. After paying for her groceries she suddenly realized that she needed one more household item, a fly swatter. Immediately she let the store owner know that she wanted one that would not break on the first swat on those pesky Greek flies, like the last one she had, but one that was sturdy yet flexible and strong enough to last a full summer of fly swatting.

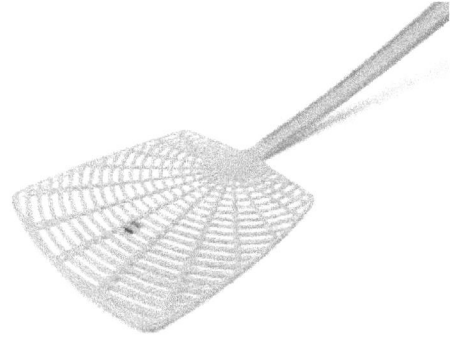

The grocery owner, listening intently to her request for such a fly swatter, quickly reached behind the counter and proudly produced the exact item she requested. Not to be bamboozled, the doubtful senior citizen wanted to see this promoted fly swatter in real action. The grocer, eager to make the sale, pointedly replied, "Just see how effectively it kills flies." Hardly were those words spoken when he spotted the nearest unfortunate fly buzzing around the Turkish delights, behind him. With one swift, deadly motion of his wrist, he smashed the fly up against the wall, leaving a dark smudge on the newly painted surface.

The customer impressed, but still not convinced of the over- all quality of the fly swatter, needed additional evidence of its destructive force. Leaping over the counter, like Superman, the grocer spotted two other possible victims flying around the store. Stealthily tracking them from the fresh fruit stand to the back of the store by the soap display, he methodically in a matter of a few seconds, proved his point twice over.

Finally convinced of the fly swatter's overall value and construction, the customer plunked down her one Euro, and proudly marched out of the store holding her groceries in one hand and brandishing her new weapon of destruction, complete with dangling parts and guts of the unfortunate flies in the other.

OTE

OTE are the three letters that represented the omnipresent Greek telephone company even on our little island of Ikaria. A neighbor of ours happened to be walking past our house cradling a phone in his arms one early morning looking rather confused and in a state of mild agitation. Noting his disposition, as a neighbor who normally is a happy go lucky kind of a guy, I immediately asked, "Why such a sullen face on such a beautiful morning?"

"Well," he said, "You know I have had my name on the list to get a land line from OTE for years. Finally, about a year ago they notified me that I was next on the list, and within a month they came and installed my phone. Since then I have had nothing but trouble and annoyance with OTE. Everything from poor phone reception, to no reception, to billing problems, but what took the cake was my ordeal with them yesterday. Once again I called OTE to complain about the spotty phone service I was receiving. I told them I would be on the phone talking, and without warning my call would be cut off. Sometimes if I stayed on the line for two or three minutes' service would resume, only to be disconnected again a few minutes later. 'Apparently', said the OTE technician while checking my line, 'your phone seems to be working fine now, what I suggest you do in the future is to call us back when your phone is not working'. I couldn't believe what I was hearing, so I just hung up on him. That's why I'm on my way to Agios to dump this junky OTE phone and get myself into the 21st century with a reliable cell phone."

This fleeting incident reminded me of the T.V. comedy "Laugh-In," back in the 60's, you might recall Lily Tomlin's character, Ernestine, as a dismissive and condescending phone operator. Her celebrated parting words at the end of each sketches were, "We don't care, we don't have to, we're the phone company."

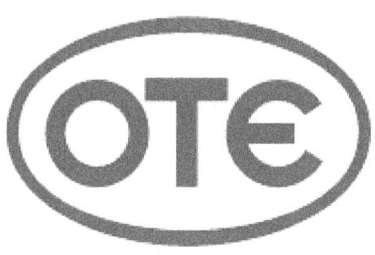

IT DID WHAT?

I am normally a sympathetic and understanding man, or at least I think I am. There are times however on Ikaria when no amount of understanding seems to fit the situation.

One of my favorite activities on Ikaria is spear fishing while enjoying the beautiful blue solitude of the world beneath the Aegean waves. In the years that I have been fishing I've caught my fair share of fish, but the prize that really thrills me the most is spearing an octopus. Catching it, pounding it on the rocks forty times, then taking it up to the house and grilling the octopus for meze, it's a delightful culinary treat that I look forward to on every trip to Ikaria. Since my first experience in spearing an octopus I've realized how intelligent these creatures are, from their varying colors of camouflage blending with their surroundings to their tactical retreat in a cloud of black ink.

Nothing however, could have prepared me for an incident that happened one peaceful afternoon. Upon entering the water with my fishing gear in tow, I followed my usual underwater path in my quest for a seafood snack. It didn't take long for me to spot a medium sized octopus sunning itself casually on a rock. Steadily and quietly I swam towards my intended prey, my spear gun cocked and the safety off. I was already envisioning a tasty octopus meze with some ouzo, olives and cheese while regaling my wife with my fishing success.

As I slowly approached within feet of my soon-to- be meze, I took careful aim and gently pulled the trigger of my gun. The spear went whizzing through the water in a matter of micro-seconds and implanted itself in the unsuspecting target. Beaming with delight and with a primitive feeling of a successful hunt, I started to pull my spear and prize back. That's when I noticed my spear tip was not implanted securely in the body of the cephalopod, but had impaled itself in several of the octopus arms. I knew that if I did not pull the octopus quickly towards me so that I could grab it, it would no doubt be able to wiggle out of the barbs of my spear tip and swim away.

The octopus meanwhile didn't just have escaping on his mind, he was going a step further. This cephalopod meant to disarm me. With unbelievable dexterity, my opponent held the spear steady with a couple of arms and with a couple of more began unscrewing counter clockwise the trident tip. I was so amazed by the agility of my opponent that I completely froze, while he continued methodically to dismantle my spear. This octopus fully understood how to take my weapon apart. How many times had he been shot I wondered. He rendered my spear useless in a matter of seconds.

With what I swear was a gleam in his eyes and a trophy in his arms, he swam away leaving me dumbfounded in his wake. Cursing the thieving octopus underwater is not as gratifying as cursing it on land I soon found out after gagging on several mouthfuls of salt water.

I swam back to shore now feeling defeated and deflated. Stumbling out of the water, still spitting out salt water, I mumbled an account of what just transpired under the waves to my disbelieving wife. Her only response was, "It did what?!"

I imagine, somewhere out there in the Aegean, this armed octopus tells all his octopus friends that grand tale of the day he bested man, and perhaps hanging over his mantle in his octopus home proudly shines my apprehended trident spear tip.

NOW WHO'S MACHO?

There is definitely no lack of machismo on Ikaria. It reveals itself by the deeds and actions of the locals in a variety of perplexing and sometimes entertaining ways. Let me be clear, it often crosses gender lines with displays of strength and virility by both sexes. Occasionally this machismo seems a bit daffy, and often personally dangerous.

Case in point would be my plumber, Nick, a man who has worked deftly with his enormous hands all his life. Looking at them your eyes are immediately drawn to his tough and callous fingers. These did not go unnoticed by my astute, young daughter, Andrea. After Nick finished a rather unpleasant and messy plumbing job in our bathroom, Nick took a much needed break and relaxed with us outside with a Greek coffee and a cigarette. Finishing our obligatory meze, and the mandatory discussion of the Greek economy, Nick got up to leave. He reached over, held his left palm out and with his enormous right hand fingers, took and crushed his still burning cigarette in his left palm. All this without hesitation and without flinching an iota. This act of machismo astonished my daughter, who couldn't believe her eyes. Did it hurt? Why did he do it? Did he feel the burn? Were all questions that popped out of her mouth.

Considering the many forest fires Ikaria has witnessed these past several years, Ikarians are very diligent about putting out any embers or flames that could potentially cause a wildfire. This was Nick's way of extinguishing his lit cigarette. A bit unorthodox, but it sure looked totally macho and bad ass to the delight of my daughter.

Physical endurance and strength have always been hallmarks of machismo. These manly acts have sometimes left me scratching my head, and wondering why people put themselves through such agonizing physical undertakings.

It wasn't that long ago that I met a young Greek-American woman living in the village about two miles from our village of Xilosirti. About twice a week I watched her walk to Agios, carrying a backpack on her journey for groceries. The walk from her village to Agios is roughly about five or six miles one way. She would take one of two ways to get there. The first is the main road that connects the villages, most of it is paved, but some parts are hilly and unproved. The second is somewhat shorter, but clearly a more challenging route. It follows the shoreline and requires one to traverse over sand, rocks and around giant boulders. It's a course that most people avoid because of the immense physical exertion it takes to climb over and under the protruding bedrock. Regardless of the dangers I often saw her take both routes and admired her physical stamina and endurance.

One day we ran into each other in our village bakery, where she had stopped for a cold drink on her way home from Agios. Her backpack was crammed full of groceries and she was carrying a good size watermelon in her hands. This chance encounter gave me the opportunity to ask her why she chose to walk those many miles for groceries, when she could just as easy call a cab or hitch a ride with one of the locals. She replied that she loves the exercise, the abundant fresh air all the while appreciating the wild beauty of Ikaria.

I commended her on her arduous jaunts for groceries, that is until I observed that around each of her ankles was fastened a five-pound ankle weight. Weights that she always wore on those long ten mile plus hikes. A kind of cardio workout that would stress any world class athlete, carrying 20-25 pounds of food while wearing ankle weights over uneven rugged terrain for mile after mile under the Greek sun. This feat still astonishes me and defines the meaning of macho regardless of gender.

As always renovations to our little house continue, and prove to be challenging macho endeavors. One of the latest, and well overdue home improvements was to replace a window between two bedrooms. This particular window at one time was part of the exterior of the house, and was enclosed in a solid steel frame. I knew this was not going to be an easy and quick upgrade, nothing like this ever is on Ikaria. My plan was to hire my Rasputin-looking mason, Elias who had replaced several windows before for us with excellent results. Upon his timely arrival, and not the two or three days later which is acceptable Ikarian time, he sized up the situation and declared he could complete the job in a day.

When the agreed upon day finally arrived I was particularly anxious to see how he would remove that troublesome steel casing. Wasting no time Elias in his pre-animated state, opened up his dusty tool bag and lifted out an enormous industrial strength grinder. I knew at that precise moment I was in for a display of supernova fireworks. I had also assumed Elias would wear some kind of protective gear while he was vigorously grinding away at the metal. I was wrong, what he wore to work that day was a light blue wife beater undershirt beneath a blue bib overall. Not exactly the outfit one expects to wear as sparks and hot cinders are flying all about. He wore no hat, no gloves, no safety goggles and no mask of any kind to cover his bushy beard. I made a feeble attempt to give him a pair of gloves and a hat, but he refused them to my consternation, claiming he has done this kind of work before without any injuries. A claim I found dubious at best. I already envisioned myself frantically running to the bathroom in search of the first aid kit, as he started up the grinder.

In no time, sparks and a black cloud of choking smoke arose from the worksite. Competing with all this noise and smoke, I often could hear a loud high pitched "whoo whoo" sound coming from Elias. Through the clouds of smoke I could make out sparks flying and landing between Elia's undershirt and his overalls. He would promptly stop cutting, and pat down the hot embers, hopping like a rabbit around the room to remove them before they burn his skin. Amazingly enough after a couple of tense hours, the job was completed without any serious bodily injuries. "See I told you I didn't need any of those safety devises," the soot covered Elias said with a smug macho grin, as the black suffocating smoke cleared out of the room. I shuttered to think what would happen if this situation occurred in the States, what would OSHA the EPA, Workman's Comp, Brian Boitano say? One thing is for sure, inevitably the bushy beard would have to go.

These typical examples of Ikarian machismo reflect the continuously arduous life on Ikaria, sometimes humorous, sometimes dangerous, but always entertaining.

IKARIA, JULY 1970

There exists an island eight to eighteen hours from Athens, but in my mind no distance exists between us. We approach her cautiously, huddled tightly together on a wet deck of a slow churning ship. She rises majestically in the distant cerulean pelagos, delicately shrouded by the dawn's early mist. Her ghostly presence stills my thoughts and races my heart. The morning fog, the temptress wind, the asperity of the mountains makes a grand entrance fit for the noblest and virtuous of kings.

Shaped by the hands of nature a collage of air, land and water, she plays, she teases, she torments the inhabitants of her body and calls out to them. "Come play with my body and I will play with your souls". She will not forsake them but in the end, survival is justified only for the living.

On the left there's the sea

On the right there's the land

And in between can be found man

Her winds whistle through the pines and race down her lonely rocky roads. Yes, I will not forsake you she whispers but in the end. Man will struggle and he shall survive with his plot of earth all within the face of time.

The village, nestled warm and snug, half way up the mountain side, revealed as a pattern of white specks, specks you could brush off your shoulder with a swipe of your hand. Your feet sing along on the winding road and in the night it becomes your captor. "Follow me," it says, "Your destiny lies in me." You follow one step after another, one thought after another, wondering about the scenes your captor has witnessed and knowing for the moment you are part of them.

The light shines, it shines low and dim in the old house with the fading whitewash. The ancient stones planted in the patio greet your weary body and lead you towards its' haven. First, the kitchen, filled with countless aromas seemingly still drifting from the cooking pots carefully arranged in the fireplace. Solid wooden benches along the walls seat visitors coming to narrate the news of the day. The three tiny bedrooms, all with icons, closely watching and protecting their human spirits, providing respite for the slumbering souls. The store room, dark and dusty, permeated forever by the scent of olive oil. On its' wall dangle the implements of survival, massive amphoras for oil, wine and water, a handmade wooden loom, and the universal tools used by farmers eons ago.

Here on this mystic isle you find love, you find hate, as you search for the dreams of man. So, in the end you too can say, "I played among those gods of the heart." The sun is always high, the moon is always bright, and the stars parade before you every night. This island my friend is your world and you shall be all right.

POKING DEATH WITH A STICK

Mrs. Milla lived alone on a tranquil Greek island, Ikaria, an island known for the longevity of its inhabitants. She was a furtive recluse of undetermined age. Her desire for privacy was of paramount concern, thus leading her to withdraw from any social affairs or functions of the village. Since her husband's passing, Mrs. Milla lived in what the locals called "The Cuckoo's Nest", an illegally built structure much like an efficiency apartment perched on top of a one car garage. Visually the place had a rather ominous and forbidding feel to it.

The miniscule room included a toilet in one corner, a sink next to a dingy refrigerator in another, and in the middle a rust-encrusted iron bed with a lumpy mattress. The room was overwhelmed by a multitude of boxes and trunks that hugged the walls of the tiny room. They were all tied and secured shut with various ropes and locks, protecting her valuables from would-be intruders, real or imaginary.

Next to "The Cuckoo's Nest" is a patio, and adjacent to it is her deceased husband's patriarchal home. A home in which she squatted much to the anguish of her husband's extended family, as they tried numerous times to evict her, unsuccessfully. This second home, or summer home as it was called by the family, through time became another depository for her boxes and containers, once again secured with heavy chains, ropes, and locks. It was well known through village gossip that her illegal occupation of the summer home resulted in its premature dilapidation. The bathroom of the home became useless as pipes rusted and disintegrated and the toilet became obstructed by years of accumulated trash. That house also took on a musty, irritating odor of expired life.

When she was seen in the village it was only to go to the small grocery store, pulling her wobbly shopping cart. She never left her home without being fully dolled up in a way that showed her faded charm and worldly ways. Her signature look included a smear of bright red lipstick, an abundance of caked - on rouge, while wearing enormous sunglasses and an equally massive sunbonnet. On rare occasions we would see her walking past our house pulling her grocery cart, seemingly floating along like a decorated apparition. No one knew how she passed her time or with whom. Acquaintances were few and village friends even fewer. A distant niece in Athens was mentioned but never seen. A concerned sister-in-law, Mrs. Koula, would come by once a week and check in on her. Occasional help offered by well-meaning villagers was quickly brushed aside. Her estranged life style continued unabated year in and year out. The summer of 2019, fate stepped in and became a deviator in Mrs. Milla's life.

Our house is located a couple of hundred meters away from "The Nest". On a meltemi day, that fierce wind out of Russia, that locals say could blow the ears off a donkey, we can get a glimpse of "The Nest". Ever looming like a formidable fortress high on the garage roof. Most Sunday mornings are quiet in our village with only the church bells ringing calling to the faithful, while kids play in the church yard and men toss around the latest scuttlebutt. My wife and I were busy that clear pristine morning attending to some much neglected yard work, when I glanced up and was distracted by an ambulance quietly passing by making its way up the dusty road towards Mrs. Milla's home. Without much hesitation, but with a flurry of deliberation I turned anxiously to my wife and said, "I better go see what's going on". By the time I walked to "The Nest", two ambulance attendants dressed in white, one with an unlit cigarette clumsily clinging to his lower lip, were tacitly ushering an empty stretcher towards the patio. There in the middle of the patio laid the motionless body of Mrs. Milla bathed in the shimmering sunlight. Standing over her was Mrs. Koula, calmly conversing with the attendants who had pronounced Mrs. Milla deceased. A small sigh of relief emerged from Mrs.

Koula as she saw me approaching. "Is there anything I can do?" I asked as we all stood fixated on the body of Mrs. Milla. "I came by to check on her after church and found her laying here on the ground, still in her night gown," replied Mrs. Koula. "I think she was going for help, I really don't know." The body lying there in the bright Greek sun against a bluebird sky, seemed both natural and unnatural, as if she was sunning herself, but with eyes wide open and teeth slightly protruding.

It was at that very moment that I noticed my surroundings. The patio is a fairly large rectangular space, yet it wasn't the size that startled me but rather the shock of how it was adorned. Lined up along the sides of the patio, like soldiers on parade were twenty inverted flower pots painted blood red with ornate rocks placed on top of each one so the wind wouldn't blow them away. Scattered randomly around the patio were other rocks of various sizes and shapes all painted in a profusion of bold rainbow colors and exotic designs. Along the sides of the patio stood some half grown trees, most of them had their trunks painted robin egg blue, and attached to the branches were pink plastic ribbons. They fluttered in the wind highlighted in the morning sun, seemingly giving the patio a distinctive carnival atmosphere. In the midst of this Felliniesque scene lay the deceased body of Mrs. Milla. The scope of this psychedelic spectacle bewildered me beyond words. This death was not a random mundane occurrence. Like any work of art, life has to be questioned. I was baffled by the bright colored flower pots, streaming ribbons, painted trees and rocks along with the departed Mrs. Milla. I tried to envision and get a sense of what she was trying to artistically convey, was this just a frivolous exercise of the obscure, or a huge well-orchestrated art piece. My mind labored desperately for some sort of answer, but at last none materialized.

Meanwhile, two of Mrs. Milla's nonagenarian brothers-in-law, who had accompanied Mrs. Koula from church that morning slowly came to the realization that Mrs. Milla had passed. One of the brothers-in-law, Tony, Mrs. Koula's husband, sat motionless outside on the patio wall gazing off into the far distance. He had his back turned, not even venturing to take a peek at his deceased sister-in-law, perhaps in fear that maybe the grim reaper might find him and call him home too. George, the other brother-in-law, granite faced and with years of hard living behind him, showed no such fear. He traversed gingerly down the patio steps, wooden cane in his trembling hand to view his sister-in-law. Standing staunchly over her, and gazing suspiciously down at the motionless body, he unexpectedly raised his cane and started poking vigorously at the side of the corpse, like a curious kid poking at a roadside kill. "She's dead", I said deliberately, but being hard of hearing he continued his incessant poking. Again, in a louder voice, trying to redirect him, I said: You don't have to do that, she is dead". Finally, after a couple more emphatic pokes, a slight nod of his head, and a whispered "May God forgive her," he turned and with cane in hand walked back up the stairs.

For a brief moment the two stoic ambulance attendants, now fervently smoking their cigarettes, seemed stunned by this garish scene. Regretfully unprepared to carry out their duties, they asked us for a sheet to cover the body and some form of identification of the deceased. Mrs. Koula and I wasted no time and promptly entered the darken summer home in search of those elusive items. I muddled around the dingy front room, repeatedly tripping over locked suitcases and boxes, while Mrs. Koula bravely ventured into the dark back bedroom. A short while later she emerged with a huge key ring that held at least a couple dozen varied size keys, and after trying half of them she was able to finally unlock one of the dressers. She swiftly produced a clean white sheet. While searching the dresser she surprisingly found Mrs. Milla's American passport along with a purse that contained a small amount of money. Taking the sheet the ambulance attendants respectfully covered the body, placed it gently on the stretcher, and wheeled it towards the waiting ambulance. I followed closely behind when I heard one of the attendants say in subtle but exacting voice, "Someone has to follow us to the morgue to complete the necessary paperwork". Mrs. Koula, being a kind-hearted and trusting relative volunteered as we cautiously climbed the stairs. Tony, meanwhile, looking famished was still sitting on the patio wall with his back facing the fateful scene. Seeing his wife he blurted out in a petulant voice, "When are we going to eat? I'm getting hungry". Not missing a beat Mrs. Koula with a cryptic reply, "Well, you know your sister-in-law hasn't eaten either and she's hungry". Looking at each other Mrs. Koula and I instantly broke out in a tension releasing laugh. Her husband contemplating what his wife was going to serve for lunch that day sat there silently in the deep dark shade.

The ambulance turned and discreetly made its way down the road towards the morgue with Mrs. Koula following behind in her car. She was accompanied by the vacillating chirping of the cicadas, as if performing a death dirge. With nothing else to do I headed home. As I walked past hungry Tony and under the shadow of "The Cuckoo's Nest" the heat pressed on my eyes, and the air grew stifling. My walk was measured as my mind started buzzing from the morning's bizarre series of events and the mix of all the eccentric characters and sights. It seems that poking death with a stick, both literally and figuratively is a common human condition, especially as we age and the specter of death emerges as a real possibility. We poke death with an assortment of actions and with our thoughts and ask questions. "Why does this happen? How do we face death?" Or the refusal to even contemplate the possibility of death. These are questions that have been asked by humans for millennium. Mrs. Milla seemed to have answered those questions in creating comfort for her body and soul. She constructed an elaborate backdrop expressing herself through the colorful, yet bizarre surroundings she created, perhaps leaving us a message as she waited for death's arrival. We all create our own meaningful environs as we wait ultimately for the final day, be it surrounded by religious symbols and ceremonies or the quiet gathering of family and friends, or the lonely quietude of just ourselves. When the poking finally stops so do our living years.

HOW POLITICAL IS YOUR BEER?

Beer, that ubiquitous brewed beverage that cools your thirst and fills your belly has been consumed and enjoyed by humans for thousands of years. The Egyptians over 4,000 years ago drank copious amounts of beer as they were busy constructing the Great Pyramids. During the Medieval Ages people drank it to avoid the various plagues and diseases that scourged much of Europe. Much later in the 17th. century beer thirsty European settlers introduced large scale brewing to the New World.

Ikarians today also are no strangers to beer. Especially on those hot, dry summer days when only a cold beer will suffice to quench one's thirst, or in the evening enjoying a plate of souvlaki with a companion bottle of one's favorite beer. Beer has also played a unique and seemingly peculiar role in Ikarian politics.

Politically Ikarians span the political spectrum, but for the most part lean to the left. At one time Ikaria was known as the "Red Rock" because of the abundance of Socialist and Communist sympathizers, who routinely voted for either the Socialist or the Communist politicians both locally and nationally. Political discussions in the coffee houses during an election year are always heated, passionate and loud to the point where friends who were lifelong companions terminated friendships over mundane or nonsensical political disagreements.

It was during one of these heated political arguments in our local coffee house, I noticed the verbal combatants drinking their favorite beers as they took a break from their fiery discussions. A sharp beer disparity clearly emerged among the debaters, as different as any social or political disagreement. The supporters of the Panhellenic Socialist Movement (PASOK) who's political emblem is green and white only drank Heineken beer, a bottle that happens to be a dark green color. Meanwhile, the Communist Party of Greece (KKE) were all drinking Amstel beer which is in a red bottle, the same red as the Communist emblem. Coincidence, I thought, that the members of each political party drink their beer in accordance with the color of the beer bottle that matches the color of their political party. It wasn't till sometime later I noticed the same people in local restaurants frequently drinking the same politically correct beers. Once again proclaiming publicly their allegiance to their party by the color of their beer bottle. I was further confused when I saw a few patrons drinking Alfa beer which has both green and red on its label. I wondered if this is for people who can't make up their minds as to which political party they belong to, being wishy-washy migrating from one political party to another, or maybe they just prefer the taste of Alfa beer over all others.

Now, with the proliferation of craft beers, with their colorful beer labels and emblems, how is an Ikarian to choose one's politically correct beer? Will atonements have to be made? Allegiances altered? Regardless, Ikarians will still drink their beer and maybe now with the availability of these new brews political discussions will still be heated, but maybe in a gentler, more tranquil way.

ONE MORE FORM…

It was time. The iconic red Vespa that fashionably transported me all around Ikaria for more than thirty years, had reached its terminal end. It had been relegated as a backup mode of transportation now that car rentals were so widely available and affordable on the island. So, with nostalgic bittersweet feelings, I decided to finally sell my faithful two wheeled transport.

Little did I know that selling the Vespa would require a Herculean effort on my part as well as on the part of the buyer. I should have known better based on my past experience with the infamous Greek bureaucracy, that nothing in Greece is impossible, but everything is difficult. The selling and the new registration would require two summers of paperwork to complete.

Beginning in the summer of 2022, my niece's husband, Yanni, became a very willing buyer and offered cash for the Vespa. Once a price was negotiated the paper work began in earnest. Since I was a part time resident of Ikaria, I never thought to insure the bike or pay the yearly road tax as I should have done. It came as no surprise when Yanni mentioned that the first order of business was to insure the bike. I tracked down the insurance office/travel agency, where you could buy a boat ticket or a variety of cheap tourist trinkets, while at the same time insuring your vehicle. After three visits to this muti-faceted office to acquire and fill out the correct forms, the Vespa was finally insured. The rest of the summer was spent on procuring the road tax forms and paying the tax on the bike, something I hadn't done since 1985.

I was constantly fretting, as I tried to figure out how much road tax I would have to pay, plus interest and penalties for avoiding the road tax for thirty seven years. Luckily, avoiding taxes in any form is a national pastime for most Greeks. I was fortunate that a recently enacted law stated that only the past five years of delinquent road tax would have to be paid. A sum that for me came to under fifty Euros. With the summer in Ikaria coming to an end I felt pleased and confident that I had achieved two major accomplishments and looked forward to completing the transfer of the Vespa the next summer.

Arriving in Ikaria the summer of 2023, I anxiously looked forward to the conclusion of the Vespa saga. Once again I was startled by the cumulative layers of Greek bureaucracy, as I tried gallantly to transfer the title and registration of the Vespa. The process commenced with Yanni and myself appearing at the police station to obtain the transfer forms. A simple procedure, I noted with glee, as the police officer gave us the forms to fill out right there at the station. A series of unrelated questions about my family history threw me off at first, but the forms were completed and turned in to the presiding officer. Quickly accepting the paperwork, he turned to us and said. " I need to see the bike." We had not anticipated that the Vespa had to make a personal appearance. "I need to see that the motor vehicle numbers match with the ones you stated on these forms," the officer said in a matter of fact voice. So much for our first foray, we turned and walked away pledging to bring the Vespa another day.

Returning to the police station several days later, with the Vespa in tow, Yanni and I once again made our appearance before the presiding officer. More forms had to be submitted, proof of insurance, proof that the road tax was paid,(which incidentally had to be paid at our local all purpose post office). The verification of the engine numbers progressed smoothly, all numbers matched as the officer meticulously inspected the Vespa. Returning inside, the officer proceeded to enter online our completed forms, which seemed rather redundant to me and a waste of time. Finally, he asked me for the original title and registration form from 1985, which I produced slightly soiled with grease and engine oil. After examining it closely with all the properly attached stamps, officially stamped and signed by the officiating officer back in 1985, he attached it to the growing plethora of official looking forms.

Turning to Yanni the officer said,"You need to go to the bookstore and buy a large envelope so I can enclose the forms and mail them to Samos," a nearby larger island that serves as the regional police station. Yanni already had a large envelope in which he kept his papers, and replied "I have this envelope can't you just use this one"? "No," answered the officer,"it has to be exactly like this one," holding up the correct official large brown envelope in question,with the proper elastic closure. Yanni, now perplexed, asked, "So, is there an official color of envelope I should buy?" The officer, looking none too pleased with Yanni's surly question, answered. " Just buy the envelope and bring it back to me so I can send it off" abruptly turning his back to us.

Sensing that we had semi-concluded our mission we vacated the police station and made our way to our local bookstore in search of the officially designated brown envelope with the correct elastic closure. With the approved envelope in Yanni's hand, he returned to the police station where the testy officer made sure all the forms were duly sorted, stapled and placed in the official envelope to be sent on its way to yet another bureaucratic entity. With our part done, and the Vespa finally in Yanni's possession, I felt relieved knowing the little red Vespa will enjoy its second life. That is unless during my next visit to Ikaria the Greek bureaucracy decides that the red paint color on the Vespa is not really red, but a pinkish blush color that needs additional amended forms to be filled out.

AGIOS KIRIKOS II

Agios Kirikos, the capital of our small laid-back island of ikaria is a relatively young city by Greek historical standards. It reminds me of a young acne-prone teenager, struggling valiantly to reach adulthood and respectability in a ever changing world. Agios is not an aesthetically pleasing city as picturesque Greek cities go, but granted it recently has made some remarkable strides and is trying to become a more dignified and appealing capital. Its minuscule harbor has been enlarged, spruced up and partially enclosed, protecting her from the turbulent Aegean Sea and wild meltemi winds. The epicenter and heart beat of Agios is the platea: a large open space next to the harbor crammed with traditional kafenia (coffee houses) and encircled by various small businesses, hotels and municipal offices. Veering off from the center of the platea are the numerous labyrinthian style streets extending all the way up to the neighboring village. Unfortunately, the narrow streets were made for two donkeys to safely pass each other, today it's more like two small Fiats. There are still certain stretches of city roads where I believe there are more potholes than concrete. Street maintenance seems to have remained a fleeting afterthought for the city fathers, or maybe just a matter of benign neglect.

Many new 21st century style stores have recently emerged. They include, computer and cell phone stores, a glut of nuevo type Starbuck coffee shops, mundane tourist shops, delivery stores, UPS style, to make sure the ubiquitous Amazon packages get promptly delivered. Even a tattoo parlor, that I have never seen anyone enter, has recently opened up. In spite of these cosmopolitan trappings, Agios doesn't stray much from her agrarian roots, as one can still plainly hear roosters crowing in the middle of the city. Still, it's the inhabitants of a city that ultimately determine the milieu and Agios is no different. A typical summer day in Agios finds the city full of commercial trade, but with a particular twist in that its citizens exhibit a definite laissez-faire attitude. The day would start early in the platea, but not too early, except for the young blurry eyed revelers usually under the age of 21. They come into Agios after spending the night partying at the local hang out, the Wawa where if you are over 21 you are already an old fart. They come into town looking for a double Greek coffee, an iced frappe or a tiropita (cheese pie), before heading home for some much-needed sleep.

A short time later, eager-eyed tourists flock to the coffee houses for their fix of coffee, gazing at unfolded maps of the island, checking to see which attraction or beach to hit that day. The courageous or more often than not naive tourists rent cars and motorbikes believing that the roads shown on their maps are paved, but in reality only major ones are and only partially. They will soon encounter dangerous gravel mountain switchbacks, precarious cliffs, and the ever present wild ravenous mountain goats, that outnumber the local inhabitants almost two to one. By this time store owners are slowly opening their shops as delivery guys make their rounds using an assortment of vehicles, motorbikes, scooters, vans, trucks, dollies, every mode of transportation, except mules and donkeys. The local fishmonger holding a plastic bag filled with his nightly catch yells out what fish he has available as he makes his customary rounds. Never in a big hurry he often stops by for a coffee and a chat as the fish in the bag are slowly being almost parboiled by the morning heat.

Later, old men come pondering ritualistically into the kafenia, massaging their worry beads as they greet each other in familiar ways. They take their accustomed seats at the wobbly tables as the waitresses already know what kind of coffee each man wants. This social gathering of men happens every morning, chitchatting centers about politics, sports, health issues or just plain gossip. Off to the fringes of the kafenia there are always a few men that meet to play a highly pleasurable, but competitive game of tavli (backgammon) usually in total silence.

So, as the morning wears on the sounds of smacking tavli chips and roosters crowing permeate the morning air. Late morning to early afternoon, cars are now flooding the narrow streets of Agios creating immediate traffic jams. Nervy drivers search desperately for a coveted parking spot as close to their favorite grocery store as possible, often acting like temperamental Greek gods. At the banks and pharmacies customers are anxiously queuing up to pay a bill or pick up their meds, scanning intensely for some shade to stand in while they wait patiently outside. The kafenia by now have become de facto offices for many as business deals are hashed out and agreed upon, and working arrangements are discussed over yet another cup of Greek coffee. Meanwhile, a slew of dazed looking citizens, clutching reams of official looking papers, shuffle slowly and methodically from one municipal office to another. The hope is to resolve the never-ending issues of taxes, overdue bills or property matters that need another government seal or one more official signature.

By mid afternoon, Agios slows down as people make their way home for the big meal of the day and then maybe a quick siesta. I remember many years ago when Agios would shut down completely in the late afternoon by an official decree. For about three hours stores would be closed, no vehicles were allowed on the street, and a chain was placed across the main street to keep cars from entering the city. Today things are different as the crowds leave the stores and kafenia there are still stragglers hanging around. They are soon to be joined by sun-drenched, thirsty tourists, looking for a late lunch or to guzzle down a gallon of cold water after spending hours on the beaches. The relentless Greek heat is so hot it makes their faces look like Salvador Dali's melting clocks painting. Even shopkeepers appreciate this downtime to relax a bit, do some restocking or catch up on the latest gossip.

As night settles in, Agios really comes alive. In the distance, one sees the islands of Fourni seemingly floating effortlessly in the Aegean with a warm pinkish glow shrouding the islands against the purple hazy sky. Usually around 8 PM entire families come to stroll around the platea stopping for a light meze or ice cream. The kids by now have made the platea their playground, riding their bikes or scooters, playing soccer or just plain running around. It is not unusual to see young kids, 5, 6 or 7 years old, playing with their friends away from their parents way past 10 PM, secure in the knowledge that everyone looks after the safety of the children. At the other end of the platea are the ever-present lovers arm in arm slowly promenading from one end to the other while avoiding the onslaught of darting children on scooters. If there's a soccer match or basketball game on TV, the kafenia owners will wheel out their large TVs, place them in front of their stores so locals can sit outside to watch the game and hopefully order a drink or a meze or two. Meanwhile, in what seems like a designated spot at the edge of the platea teenagers gather tightly in small groups resembling a rugby scrum. Their phones securely attached to their hands hanging awkwardly like an extended appendage, sharing the latest videos or photos. Calls and texts are made to other friends setting up rendezvous times usually at the Wawa for nocturnal activities.

The roosters are now down for the night, but the crowing is replaced by the drowning noise of motorbikes driven by young males as they roar down the perimeter streets of the platea. It seems the object of this nightly excursion is to see who has the loudest, muffler-lacking bike, presumably to impress the young teenage girls. By around midnight, people start making their way home, abandoning the comfort of their kafenio chairs after having consumed one too many ouzos or that triple scoop of ice cream. The kids are finally worn out from all the playing, but still eager to continue frolicking on the platea as their parents try valiantly to rein them in.

These are the enchanted times when Agios surfaces and resembles a Hallmark movie, comfortable, familiar, strangely entertaining, relaxed with a genial air. Agios truly exemplifies the celebrated laid-back attitude of Ikaria where it could take up to half an hour to pick out a new broom or just as long to drive from one end of the city to the other. All this encased in the ever-spirited and intoxicating enjoyment of a full Ikarian lifestyle.

Photo taken by Julie Hardaloupas

THREE CHAIRS AND A TABLE

A people's character develops from the spirit of place, as Lawrence Durrell reminds us. To that I would add, whole heartedly, the spirit of time. It is this symbiotic combination of the two, time and place, that creates the character of the people whom we come to love, respect, admire, or even loathe as we pass on our long terrestrial voyage.

The summers I spend on the Blue Zone island of Ikaria, Greece with Ikarians are stepping stones that sometimes I happily stumble over on my life's journey. Ikarians take life slowly, indulge in the joys of the day, reflect on the past, and cautiously approach the future. This basic philosophy is best exemplified by important time tested daily rituals in our small village. These familiar rituals are honored year after year, generation after generation, as the human symphony plays on.

An essential ritual for me is the daily excursion to our miniscule grocery store. Athena, the proprietress of the mini-market, with the voice of an earth bound angel, runs the little store in a confined but well organized manner. There you can find both frozen and fresh foods, personal care items, household goods, a postal service, and of course the customary variety of alcoholic beverages. The locals, all dedicated shoppers, fully support the mini-market, in fear that someday Athena might just decide to close the store, and leave the village without a single outlet in which to buy their daily vittles, alcohol or condoms.

Her store is more than brick and mortar and merchandise. It resonates with the daily influx of customers, and times of no customers. A vital life component are the regulars who congregate communally every morning outside the mini-market. The usual assemblage includes three elderly males blithely holding royal court, seated in what seemed like a well established seating arrangement on three rickety chairs next to a rust-covered table.

I approached the mini-market one hot blistering mid-morning, the sun already roasting me like a rotisserie chicken and my head a bit dazed after a night of howling meltemi winds. There was the smell of spiced heat in the air infused with rosemary and other maquis plants. I arrived in time to see the elders getting ready to quench their daily thirst with their second bottle of Amstel beer, which I learned later was their morning limit. They had already taken care of their farm animals, done some daily gardening chores, and now it was time to gather for the morning convocation. I was quickly greeted by George, the outspoken skipper of the group. A man with a bioluminescent face, piercing brown eyes, and a smile as broad as the Mediterranean. "Got time for a beer?" he asked. "It's a bit early in the day for me," I replied, "but maybe I could join you for a while." "Well, you can't join us as a full member yet, since you are still rather young," he said in a campy kind of way. At that time I was in my early sixties, those octogenarians had at least a generation plus on me.

Stamati, the oldest, a goat shepherd with a crippling hip, was raised on the craggy mountains of Ikaria. He was sitting leaning nervously on his home made walking stick. Looking at me with a sage penetrating gaze, he finally asked. "You're Yianni Mantakounis' boy?" "Yes, I'm Dimitri," I replied rather suspiciously. " I knew your father well", he continued, "always a hard worker from sun up to sun down, transporting goods all over the island , never seemed to slow down, maybe for a quick coffee or a glass of ouzo, such a good man" "Yes, I said, he loved Ikaria and came back every chance he could get. I wish he could have made a few more trips before he passed away." In no time a slew of family stories about my father, mother and grandmother were re-hashed by Stamati. Some sad, some humorous and some mixed up in a curious sort of way. I thought to myself, because they remember him, they possess him, and he belongs to them.

"Come on, have a beer" croaked George again, "errands can wait till later." "Sure, why not?" I said, thinking I could dawdle a bit longer. Hearing this the ever vigilant Athena brought out a cold Amstel and set it down on the wobbly table in front of me. George, sensing an agreeable ear, immediately launched into a monologue about the grape harvest with special emphasis on his tsipouro, the Greek equivalent of Italian grappa. He described in full uncompromising detail why his tsipouro is the best in all of Ikaria, and how it adds longevity to one's life, as well as to a man's sexual prowess. This discourse lasted a good twenty minutes when finally the fisherman, Niko, the quiet laconic one of the group with a corrugated face and smelling of the briny sea and beer chirped in. "Praise God, as long as I can fish, I don't care, if God gives me a few more years I'll enjoy them." "Yeah, but it's a shot of my tsipouro that gets you up every morning," countered George, laughing out loud. "It's your tsipouro that is also going to put me in my grave," Niko replied, while finishing off the last of his now warm beer. It was obvious these two had years of repartee and fully enjoyed the duet of back answers on a daily basis.

Leaning forward precariously in his unsteady chair, George reached out with his callous hand and tapped me on the arm as he continued. "We inherited these seats of wisdom or gossip as some villagers claim from our predecessors about seven years ago, after the last one, old Spiro, bless his soul, passed away. His stubborn ass mule kicked him in the head, landed him in a coma and he died three days later. Can you believe that damn mule is still alive and kicking today? He pressed on with a sense of premonition "So, here we are temporary custodians of these chairs, until our time runs out, then it will be your turn, your time. You'll come here to gaze around at the beauty and wonderment of this place, the mountains, the sea. Feel the wind on your face and the sun in your eyes, have a beer, talk to the customers and tourists, deliberate the latest scandals, and political shenanigans, relive the old days, occasionally exaggerate your youthful exploits and maybe give a thought or two to the forebears you replaced." He stopped suddenly in mid sentence, turned guardedly around, slowly lifting his head and looked at his mates now deep in their own sublime thoughts. A thin smile formed and tracked across his face, and what seemed like a tear gently trickled down his sun tanned cheek and bounced off his beer bottle.

They occupy this modest place of three chairs and a table on this sage and thyme scented landscape. Time brings them a sense of peaceful continuity without false regrets. Friends bandaged together celebrating life and memories, knowing that each one has consumed a life worth living.

Later that same evening, I found myself sitting serenely under our pergola enjoying a glass of George's inspiring tsipouro and feeling the warm burn as it leisurely traversed down my throat. Contemplating the time when I too will joyfully accede to one of the three chairs. The panorama of my friends has always been wide and varied. Who among them would I ritualistically share a beer with everyday, which wobbly chair would I occupy in the seating arrangement, which personal pleasurable stories would I repeat to the mingling onlookers, which life lessons would I blissfully pass along, and finally whom would I relinquish my chair to as my time wanes and winds down? The fact that I am a product sprouted of this island gives me solace knowing that I too have an adoration of this life, in this place, at this time.

Biography of Dimitri (Jim) Mantakounis

Born in the middle part of the 20th century on the Greek island of Ikaria, Dimitri immigrated to America at the age of five with his parents who saw their future tied to the seductive "American Dream." His formative years were spent growing up in Gary, Indiana. Dimitri graduated from Indiana University with a Master's degree in education and moved to Grand Rapids, Michigan with his wife Janet. During the 1980's, son Alex and daughter Andrea entered his life and were included with his return to Ikaria every other summer. After thirty seven years of teaching, he retired along the way having published educational material, and currently writes about his beloved Ikaria on his blog www.yiasouikaria.blogspot.com.

Biography of Kemon Lardas

Kemon Lardas is a native of Pittsburgh, Pennsylvania and has many family and friend ties to Ikaria, Greece. He is an Art Institute graduate and worked until his retirement at the Carnegie Museum of Natural History Exhibits Department in Pittsburgh, where he assisted and prepared exhibits, and specialized in silk screen graphics and reproductions. He enjoys spending time with his wife Popie, his grandchildren and an occasional round of golf.

www.ingramcontent.com/pod-product-compliance
Lightning Source LLC
Chambersburg PA
CBHW050041080526
44586CB00014B/1406